planbeditorial

How Can I be a good partner?

A method to be, to look for and to keep a good partner

planbeditorial

HOW CAN I BE A GOOD PARTNER?

Belkis Carrillo @psicoespacio

ISBN: 9781985492165
Legal deposit: DC2017000584

Editorial coordination
Julio Aguilar @julioaguilar300

Design and diagramming
Luis Mariano Garcías @booksmakers

Cover design
Castor Carmona @CastorCarmona

First edition. April 2017

The beliefs that lead us to erroneous thinking are trapped in phrases that we repeat on a daily basis.

If I have to stop being what I want to love someone else, that can be anything, else, but it is not love.

Why do I keep close to me someone who does not love me well?

Time improves good relationships, but worsens to the extreme the relations that are bad.

When I ask someone to change something that makes that person happy, I am not loving that person.

Where there is humiliation, sacrifice or begging, there isn't love, but a desire for power and control.

I always try to get my patients to ask me "why am I in this relationship?"

Belkis Carrillo
@psicoespacio

Content

Words

Gifts

Service

Time

Physical contact

What tendency helps me to be a good partner: ¿aggressive or submissive?

How can we be assertive?

Step 1

Step 2

Step 3

Being desirable or lovable? Which is better?

What makes me gain love? Being a genuine person or a fake?

Distrust: when we think that watching over is loving.

To look for, not to find

The “non-negotiables”

The “where” is important when we are looking for a partner.

Men and women are different. ¿Can we accept this and love?

Women are anecdotic and men are forgetful

Women are multifocal and men are unifocal

Foreword

The decision to go to a psychologist is not an easy task. Sometimes, the last to find out that we need a therapist are us, the potential patients who through direct and indirect comments of family and friends, finally accept that "maybe" a psychologist could help us to get over, face, accept and even solve some issues of our emotional and behavioral life.

That first step, that is, to accept that we need help from a psychologist, is a very difficult one and leads us to the second step which is equally complicated: ¿who will be my psychologist? Who am "I" going to tell my problems to? My intimate thoughts? Will people think I am crazy? That I lost my balance? An infinite number of doubts that sometimes make us discard the idea of seeking expert help from a specialist. Besides, it is better to just have some coffee or scotch with friends. Friends understand us and will give us good advice. They know all our life details and only want what is best for us.

If you identify yourself with these lines of thinking, you are not alone. Almost everybody has walked that path. A long time ago, I used to think that way too, but some tangles present in ordinary lives made me go more than once to the sofa. I admit it, but I am also proud of it. The path to get over a mourning, for example, was much easier to bare thanks to a psychologist. I owe my psychologist the tools to make it easier for me to effectively communicate with my partner and with my son.

Thus, psychologists play a very important role in the development of society's emotional health, since everybody, whether we like it or not, at some point in time will have to face impacts and losses that are a part of life itself, and not all of us know how to handle our emotions.

If we go to the cardiologist when we suspect that we have a heart problem, ¿why is it so hard to visit a psychologist when behavior and emotions are involved?

According to Belkis Carrillo, the author of this book, the appointment with the psychologist arrives when the patient is already in a crisis, and as time goes on, that person that we are told can solve everything, hasn't solved the problem that really mortifies the patient.

In my experience, the sooner we look for help the better off we are. We gain time and we suffer less. It goes without saying that the psychologist must be well selected since we think of our therapist as a friend and confident, the person who will always say we are right, and that is also going to support us in our belief that our ex is a monster and that we are the victims. That the other person is at fault and not us. Poor ME, I deserve everything because I am good, hardworking, faithful and a very long list of etcetera's. If you, my reader friend, want a psychologist with these characteristics, don't call the author of this book.

I personally like the professional style of the author. Absolutely modern and revolutionary. With Belkis Carrillo, we have stepped up from the intimidating sofa to more friendly and relaxing environments that favor deep conversations, without sweeteners, firm and with the most important ingredient: solutions.

Belkis represents a new era, the new psychology, dynamic, transparent, tearing down archaic patterns that have caused a lot of suffering to many people. But Belkis is not your friend. She is your psychologist. If you can handle that, she is the best. I know, because I am her patient.

Lourdes Ubieta
Journalist – Internationalist

Dedication

This book is dedicated to the memory of one of the persons whom I have loved the most in my life: my father. My great daddy, my spoiled Juan Carrillo Mendoza, who with his infinite love for my mother taught me that good and committed men do exist.

To my mommy Ana de Carrillo, who always fomented in me with her exemplary conduct, that, to communicate and laugh together, are the best existing ways to love.

To Ale, my daughter, my friend, my buddy; to be her confident has been a wonderful school for me.

To Cayi, my son, who with his endless energy has challenged me to understand and to learn from those special beings like him, to whom life can never say NO.

To my brothers Giova, Juanchi, Gil and Alejandro who have always believed in me and have unconditionally loved me, giving me their support in good and bad times.

To my "good and bad" partners, because without them I would have never known both love and lack of love. Today they are all a part of my growth as a woman and a psychology professional.

To my patients, because thanks to the trust they placed in me, their stories and screams for help, I now have the knowledge, the experience and the curiosity incentive of which you will read about in the following pages.

And finally, to all those adults who were children sometime in the past and who learned that love is equal to pain, and that today however, they want to learn to do it in a different way, to change the paradigm and to be a happy couple.

It is not the same to make use of the right to reciprocity than to explore love.

One enriches us and the other shames us.

Water Riso

For Starters

This book emerged the moment I began to be conscious of my life. I grew up in a family that I had supposed was normal, well constituted: father, mother and two brothers. My father was a worker and my mother took care of us on a full-time basis. They got along just fine, I always perceived between them a very fun and sexual conduct, they liked each other, maybe that is why I am so extroverted and friendly in my partner relationships. I grew up seeing that and believing it was the right way.

My brothers and I had the advantage of being poor when we were kids. An advantage? Let me tell you why I saw it as an advantage. My parents were very young and didn't have money to buy or rent a house. Thanks to this reason we could live with different families during our childhood. First, we lived in an apartment with my maternal grandparents and my three uncles. There I could observe how my grandparents-whom I loved- couldn't stand each other, all due to my grandfather's infidelities when he was young. Nine years later we moved away from Caracas where life had become complicated and dangerous. My uncle would constantly hit my aunt, he would give her cigarette burns so that she could not use short clothing and frequently insulted her. I did not understand what was happening because the example I had were my parents and they were totally different.

After a few months and to keep us from seeing all those situations, my father finally bought what would be our home: a very small apartment in my home town with only one bathroom for five people and for which we had to take turns in the morning, and wait for it to be available, in the living room. We enjoyed those moments because they would allow us to talk about the events that had occurred the day before or about what we were planning on doing that day, and at the same time, to know about my father and mother. That is why communication has always been a part of my life and of my relationships. That situation with my uncle and aunt as well as my grandparents made me understand that there are people who are different, that don't wish each other well and even in a harmful way. That is why I mentioned at the beginning, that, in my case, poverty had been an advantage because it aroused this curiosity that now gives purpose to my life.

This is how I became a curious observer and, every time as soon as I arrived somewhere, I immediately started observing how people got along, but that didn't make me an expert in perfect relationships; on the contrary, I received many impacts in my life as far as partners and couple relationships is concerned. I have learned the hard way; I got divorced and I had to understand what I was doing wrong and why I was blaming a man for my life as a couple to be a complete disaster.

On top of everything, I grew in a home where my father did everything: he managed the household, he paid the bills, he bought all the supplies and groceries, among other things.

When I got married, I expected my husband to do it all, but I married a man whose mother was in charge of everything, and he expected me to act the same way. You can imagine what happened. In the words of my therapist at the time, the marvelous Romulo Aponte Baca, I was a little girl without boundaries, daughter of an extremely pleasing father: the girl who wanted everything, obtained everything and even then, she was not satisfied. And he was a subjugated child, a submissed child constantly criticized by his mother. After that, he became a man capable of making any woman who crossed his life pay for what his mother had done to him.

And there I was, the little spoiled and capricious girl to whom her father couldn't say NO, married to the rude and resented boy son of a spoiling father and of an absent and castrating mother. To get a divorce was a very hard impact for me because I always thought I could do anything, that I was going to make him change and besides, I had a lot of fears back then: fear of being left alone, fear of not being able to find another partner and to believe that nobody would want me with two kids, fear of not being able to keep up with my expenses, fear of not being capable of raising adequately my children. In other words, I was afraid I couldn't live without him: it sounds like a paradox, ¿doesn't it? I DID NOT want to live without the man who hurt me because I was afraid I would miss him and to be sorry not to have waited for him "to change" and to love me well. However, with therapeutic work, my family and close friends' support, along with watching my children grow happily, I understood that when someone doesn't love you, a divorce becomes a blessing.

I understood that most of the times we suffer because we are a bad combination and when you can see this, then half of the problem has been solved: "it is not him, it is not me, it's that our lives, our values, our laughs, our sadnesses and even our hobbies are different." That was a great schooling for me, and I believe that if that relationship hadn't been that way, if I hadn't put up with so much infidelity, lies and selfishness coming from that man, I wouldn't have read so many psychology books, I wouldn't have gone to college and I wouldn't be writing these pages. To all the pain and errors of that marriage I owe the woman I am today.

After that relation, I focused on being better every day, in understanding that I was wrong, on what I had to do in order to avoid making the same errors again, which were my worst defects, my limiting beliefs concerning love, and specially, to get to know my relationship with myself. This was particularly fruitful. All along these years, I have learned that all my fears, as a consequence of my divorce, were only the product of having stayed for too long in a place where I was not loved the way I wanted to be loved. Today, when I write these lines and I see the result of being brave, I realize that I am back to being happy in a couple and that I still am an attractive woman both physical and intellectually in spite of the fact of being divorced with two children. I have loved, I have been loved and I have had fun. I have worked both in Venezuela and abroad in several media and with very many people. I have always been able to pay my bills, my tuitions and even a few indulgencies. In other words, nothing happened the way I had imagined at that moment of vulnerability. Everything turned out just fine and it still does, just as they turn out when you show love and respect.

I will always be a believer in good love; that love that I learned to live by seeing how my parents loved each other. Up to this date, I still believe that the ideal state is to be in love with yourself and that this would allow you to look for someone who does not give you any less of what you give yourself.

And that is precisely this story, my story, what motivates me to share all of this knowledge with my readers. This is to show you that one can learn how to be a better person and to have healthy beliefs about love and relationships. By the same token, you can learn how to look for a better partner who represents an adequate combination for you, knowing you and not accepting any less of what you know you want, and finally to learn how to maintain healthy relationships where the equilibrium between giving and receiving is the golden rule.

B.C.

Those things that DO NOT make us a good partner

To have irrational beliefs about love

To be a controlling person

To be a manipulating person

To be a distrustful person

To have the wrong language before love

To have difficulties to communicate

To find and not to look for

To disrespect oneself

Not knowing your non-negotiables

Not knowing or not wanting to give

To incorrect use of the word "should"

Irrational beliefs

Let us start by checking our most negative aspects, those things we know we are doing wrong. I suggest you write them down.

Irrational beliefs about love

As we grow, we acquire experiences that are accompanied by emotions like fear, anger, sadness, happiness, etc., and the more intense the emotion, the more we believe that what happened "is going to happen again exactly the same way" in future occasions, and at that moment, a belief is generated.

I remember the case of a patient who found very difficult to trust men. She said that they were all bad and that they were born that way. After a few sessions, she "remembered" how she had fixed this belief that she had also transformed in a rule by which she claimed it would turn out the same way in 100% of the time. This girl remembered that one day after arriving from school -when she was 7 years old- found her father giving oral sex to her sister who was helplessly crying. She recalled how her sister was asking her father to stop, but he didn't. The intensity of the negative emotion she felt while watching that scene fixed in her automatic negative thought that all men are bad in essence and thought to herself: "if this man, who should love my sister, is capable of hurting her, then the other men must be worse."

To live with certain beliefs is harmful because not all are true. What I consider to be worse is that they are formed and become a magnet that will "attract" those that confirm our theories. We will go around the world finding people who will help us to be in that zone where the reason can be on our side. It is for that reason that my patient only came across, and chose, unfaithful men who would mistreat her; who would allow her to tell herself and to the world, once and again:" you see? I am right. All men are bad." And if for any reason she would find a good man who would want to really love her well, she would immediately enter a distrust zone before all of his attentions and details and was capable of promoting mislove to confirm her theory. Most of the time, this is not done at a conscious level. That is dangerous. We walk through life without realizing that the beliefs are the combination that allows us to make something wonderful and enjoyable with of our lives, or, all contraire, a place where we will feel ashamed and will want to escape. We live with many irrational beliefs about love and I call them that way because they produce pain and bring negative consequences and destruction to couples. They are beliefs based on what we hear our parents and grandparents repeat or on what we have lived and experienced at the early stages of our lives and we turn them into "laws". We stumble and get hurt once and again and we find the wrong partner once and again. Those irrational beliefs are used to stay in a bad relationship, to keep away the good ones, to be distracted, to tell ourselves a bunch of wrong things and to face the world with beliefs that do not function properly.

I want to give you another example: in my house, the metal door made a very particular noise. I knew that this noise meant that my father had arrived, and with him, bread, milk and a sweet. My father was a man of details and he would always get home with something sweet to eat; his arrival was always something pleasant and we all ran to him. However, for people of other families and other houses, the arrival of the father meant very different things. I have been told by people who had an alcoholic father that his arrival meant to run and hide either because the mother was going to get hit or because he would destroy the house. The same situation of a key in a door could generate different thoughts, emotions, and conducts. It is probable that for whom the key had a negative meaning, may still have the same hostile situation, the same meaning when the sound is heard in a different situation, because that thought was anchored with a particular emotion. To me, that sound has to do with something kind and sweet.

A patient used to tell me that when her husband was taking a bath, she would search through his briefcase, looking for receipts or proof that he was seeing another woman and she asked her nine- year-old daughter to look out for when her father came out of the shower to stop searching and leave everything the way it was. ¿How do you think the life of that child as a couple is going to be? That mother doesn't know what she is doing. She is teaching her daughter that men are beings not worthy of our trust and that we women must look for something in their things and be aware of everything they do to know if they are cheating on us. It is very likely that tomorrow that little girl will be a jealous woman and will not be able to trust men because she will be repeating a pattern that her mother taught her; a woman who forgot that we are the models for our children.

The beliefs that lead us to a wrong thinking are trapped in phrases that we repeat on a daily basis without knowing exactly what they mean. Let's see some.

Phrases about love

It doesn't matter my dear, it is ok if he doesn't change. One is willing to endure anything for love. Love makes everything possible.

¡Of course that it matters, and very much so! That a person has conducts that bother me or that hurt me and that the person doesn't even consider analyzing them and coming to an agreement, is like a torture. Then, ¡¿how can it be that they are repeated in such a cold and easy manner?! Yes, it matters that he/she doesn't change. Yes; ¡change matters! Because that makes you unhappy. So, as of today, I want you to keep in your mind that every time you repeat this phrase. you join the group of unhappy people that choose to avoid reality to stay "in a couple" in spite of the fact that this is a lie. If we stop in the phrase "to endure anything", we realize that it is some kind of self-sentencing, that it is negative and that the concept of love is sick. Look into your past and you will learn who you learned this irrationality from; accept that that person did the best she could and try to change the belief. Remember: it does matter.

We have heard this so many times from our mothers and grandmothers throughout the years that we believe it is true. However, nowadays the divorce and "fake marriages" rate (that I call those marriages between people who signed a piece of paper but that don't talk to each other and haven't had sex in centuries), let us know that love only is not enough. That the living with a partner is nourished by many factors, including love, but it is not the only one: respect, complicity, partnership, and above all the similarities that will complete the jigsaw puzzle.

Many people put up with hits, insults and mistreatments; many stop living their lives, they stop their careers and the dreams they always had because of love. That isn't love. If I must stop being what I want to be to love someone else, that can be anything else but love. That is not real love.

A patient from Spain used to tell me that she knew her husband was homosexual, and that on top of that he also used drugs, and that she was sure that with love she would make him drop both conducts that did not allow them to be happy. ¡Blindness in capital letters! Why? Because in her house her mother had tolerated years of abuse and infidelities, trusting that with love people change, and even though that never happened, my patient chose to keep using the same formula and preferred "being loyal" to what her mother had taught her. Remember what we have always been told: a good girl/boy always obeys what the mother says. Even though the expression is very old, many men and women keep using it and they continue to repeat what they learned in their home, despite the fact that it makes them unhappy.

Another patient, a young man from Caracas, suffered very much every time he liked a woman and wanted to make her fall in love with him. ¿Why? Because in the religious school he went to, they told him repeatedly during his childhood and adolescence, that if he ever decided to enjoy his sexuality, something very bad would happen to him. What did my patient do? He had become obsessed with avoiding sex or if the desire was big enough he would succumb before it and he would take lab blood tests during months to make sure he was healthy since he was trapped in the irrational thought that he deserved a punishment and that any girl that he liked would give him HIV, in spite of the fact that he used protection and exercised extreme care. The belief that he was doing something bad and that the punishment would come later, didn't let him enjoy it. His love for God kept him from living something that would seem normal to any young man: fall in love.

There is a book I like very much, *Love is not enough,* written by Aaron T. Beck, a psychiatrist and professor from the United States, creator of the Cognitive Therapy, also known as the COGNITIVE-BEHAVIOURAL THERAPY (TCC in Spanish). There he explains how the co-existence is one of the most difficult things in life and that it cannot be only based on love. He even lists those reasons by which even people who love each other end up separated. We will talk more about this later on.

Irrational beliefs related to character

¿Am I the intolerable and controlling one or what?

*¿How many of my readers are this kind of partner? In my country, Venezuela, this kind of woman is associated with a snake (*cuaima*) that is very poisonous and agile, but it is a typical local expression to depict possessive, controlling and jealous women. And in spite of the fact that in my country it would seem correct for women to behave like this, reality indicates that the consequences are terrible. In theory-according to themselves, because there is nothing written to sup-*

port this irrational belief- "cuaimas" *define themselves as women who fight anybody, in any way, to maintain a relationship. For this reason,* "cuaimas" *are the beings who suffer the most infidelities in the world. ¿Do you know why? Because this behavior means to guard, control, check, supervise, re-question, something similar to a toxic mother. ¿How many men are willing to live with a scold and criticizing mother for a lifetime? Well, nobody does. ¿And why? Because she is closing the door to the possibility of change; she is saying: "this is the way I am. Period".*

I once spoke to a couple who came to my practice and whose reason for coming to see me was that the excessive control that he exerted over her and because of the little sex they had since he had become cold in bed and he would always arrive home late or tired. When she told me everything, she did it to try to keep away any possibility of cheating on his part. I understood that the man had left without leaving, that is, he was living with her at home but was emotionally absent. She would justify herself saying: "If one lets them do as they please, the day will come when they will be beyond control". She had imposed on him certain pre-established times for phone calls of the day, that they had to be every two or three hours otherwise a discussion was imminent; she had imposed upon him that he had to call her when he was leaving the office and even if he had to work late extra hours (this required a picture to confirm it).

In more than one occasion she called his bosses to confirm that he actually was at work, and she even went to the extent of choosing certain clothing that he could only wear when he went out with her, because "with those shirts he looked too handsome and therefore I only want him to usen them with me". *Cuaimas* cannot see that if they have to control their partner, what is really happening is that they are not being really well loved. And it would be even healthier that before interrogating their partners they asked themselves:" Am I checking his cell phone because this person has a tendency to be unfaithful or because I am not good enough, because I am not so good in bed, or because I am not so cute, or so tall, or so skinny?

We don't need to follow or pursue anybody; we do not need to watch over anybody. This will only produce tiredness and nuisance for both. What is ours is ours, and if it is not there, it isn't ours. Period.

To say *"this is how I am and no one is going to change me"* just kills relationships. No one in his right mind has sex with his/her mother or father, and if you behaved like his mother or father would, trying to control everything, the sex between you will vanish.

Irrational beliefs related with time

-We have been together for three years. I know it is a short time, but I know that with time, things will change.

¡It isn't a short time! It is 1095 days of suffering, with all of its hours and minutes.

Ask yourself ¿why do I still believe that something that hasn't happened in 1000 days is going to happen later? ¿Is it possible that on day 1001 I still may feel the same love for this person that has hurt me for such a long time? ¿Why do I keep close to me someone who doesn't love me well?

"I have been repeating the same thing to her, Doctor, and I know that at a certain point, she will understand."

¿Isn't it too tortuous to live with this uncertainty? How can you heroically bare not knowing when will that "at a certain point in time she will understand" will happen? ¿Do you really believe that someone who loves you could expose you to such a waiting period? ¿Do you believe that if you loved yourself, you would make yourself wait for someone's love that on top of everything is very unlikely to occur? Irrational beliefs and of the worst kind!

Time improves the relationships that are good, but worsens to a high degree the ones that are bad. To remain in a couple relationship mines your self-esteem and it makes clear to yourself that you are not worthy nor capable of looking for a partner who loves you well. With every day that you allow yourself to be unhappy, you increase your incapacity to get out of there. Unfortunately, the human being is capable of getting used to the worst sufferings and to keep functioning, at least externally.

With time, you begin to put up with, tolerate, to keep up with things and to bare words used when the pain is present, that is, all contraire to a healthy relationship. How can you tell you have waited too long to love yourself? How do we identify that moment? This is the time that the man starts to get home late because he doesn't want to see his wife's face or because he is better off in the street with his friends or at work, and many times ignores her, ridicules or criticizes her. This is the time when the woman is always upset and defensive, denying or negotiating with the little sex they have left. Besides, when one of the two tries to escape from the trap and asks:" what is the matter with you?" or "what is happening to us?" all you can hear is the confirmation that that relationship is in coma: "nothing is the matter" or even worse, "I don't want to talk about it". Obviously, they have been for too long in a place where they are not being well loved and that destroys anybody both physically and emotionally. It is the moment of "I don't care", "it's the same" or "where am I supposed to go anyway".

Irrational beliefs of those who believe they are very sincere

-Well my love, I have had a few partners, the one who has it the smallest. Any resemblance to reality is pure coincidence. I have heard many atrocities throughout the years. "You have it the smallest" is an expression that is repeated a lot. Women believe that, by making the man feel insecure, he will never look for another woman. Sincerity can be used to improve our relationship, but it can also make it worse.

It is very important to evaluate if that truth we are going to speak is really necessary or useful. To tell your partner that of all the men you have had he has the smallest penis, is not necessarily useful, unless you want to hurt his self-esteem and end the relationship. In that case, it would be ideal to rather talk about what other things you would like to try in bed and that would make you feel more satisfied; to talk about which sex toys or sex positions could make you enjoy more the moments of intimacy with him. Sincerity sometimes becomes an aggression if you don t evaluate first what is going to come out of your mouth. And it is always fundamental to speak from the "I". "I would like"," I would want", "I think it would be better". Never use the word "you" when you want to negotiate or try to improve something. The word "you" is not good for negotiating; the other person will immediately place a wall in between because he feels he is being judged somehow.

-You are always asking me why I am always talking to her: I talk to her because she has more interesting topics than you who are always complaining, the kids, my mother, the fingernails, you are tired, and I don't know what.

The exaggerated sincerity only impoverishes the relationship. And that woman wants to talk to her husband but she doesn't leave the house –because that is what she has chosen– and only takes care of the house chores that he believes are trivial. She closes herself to everything, she tries to start a conversation but she feels stupid and inadequate, and she concentrates on the telephone, on the children, on the friends or looks for a lover. How my dear Carlos Fraga would say: "sincerity is one thing, but sincericide is another".

Irrational beliefs that suggest blindness

-My partner confessed to me that he doesn't love me, that he doesn't feel any physical desire and doesn't feel like spending time with me. I know he loves me, but he is confused.

This is effective blindness. Not seeing, not wanting to accept the wishes or desires and needs of the other. This situation is almost always encouraged by an enormous fear of loneliness and an intense need to be right. These two components together give us as a result an obsessive love, careful and controlled, that makes the relationship be less fresh and enjoyable as time goes on.

When the wishes, desires, feelings, comments and decisions of the other are constantly ignored, it is highly likely that this will cause lack of love and distance. To believe that "he loves me, but he is confused", is absolutely irrational, because when a person is in love, the person feels it, shows it and lives it at every instant. The heartbeat, the blushing, the butterflies in the stomach and the demonstrations of affection are only some of the numerous ways that people in love use to prove it.

We must open our eyes, revise our thoughts with clarity and to observe how dependent we have become of our partner and of the need of being loved; to question why, even after hearing from our partner's lips that doesn't love us anymore, we doubt it and don't believe it. We think that the cause for the lack of love is simply the lack of love and that is all. Let's meditate on the fact that letting someone go, giving them their space they are requesting and respecting their wishes is a space for us as well, to grow, to find ourselves again and to work our fears at the same time that we evaluate what was right and what was wrong in that relationship in order to not repeat those same mistakes in the future.

-My partner is a married woman, she loves me, but at the same time she feels very sad about separating her children from their father, and just for that, she is still living with him.

Here we go with the typical case of "she lives with someone else, but she loves me". And I ask myself: "how can she do that if she doesn't love herself"?

She chooses to live with a man because she feels sorry for him. ¿How can she love you? If an adult and mature person loved you, this person would know, as all of us know, that to get something you have to give something, since everything has a price in life. If the person loves you and wants to be with you, this person will need to leave the home the person has now. If the person doesn't do it and plays to have both stories, that person doesn't love you. To stop believing in those fantasies can save you from a lot of pain. Generally, these persons never get divorced, because what they are really in love with is the comfort you give them, that you allow them to have the best of both worlds and not having to pay the price for being in a real relationship.

Irrational beliefs of our cultural heritage

-A nail drives out another nail

Nothing falser! When we end a relationship, we enter a transition period. ¿have you noticed that when we take a nail out of a wall, a hole is left where the nail used to be? It is something that doesn't look good and that we want to cover in any way possible. The same thing happens with people: a part of us is left empty, sensible, hurt, sad, with anger or anxious for affection. These states do not represent a good basis for any new couple relationship.

A patient used to tell me crying that she missed her partner too much, that they had been separated a few weeks back and that she was very anxious to see him and to be with him, but that she knew that if she went out that weekend and she met somebody she liked, just that would make her feel better: "if someone sees me and likes me, I will get over this faster". She claimed that if she could find someone to be with, she would get over how bad she was feeling. ¿Why? ¿How is that you think you can exchange one person for another as if we were talking about just changing shirts? ¿How can it be that her well-being is anchored to the fact that someone else is interested in her? ¿Is it that she is missing her ex or is it that "I am alone" is what is hurting this girl? And if someone is really interested in her "would she be really focused and open to start a new relationship with such a broken heart? No, simply because she is looking for "the other nail" to live her mourning from her previous relationship with, to get distracted and to not experience the abstinence of the one who left. And this doesn't bring good results.

Transition relationships very few times end in good results and in the majority of instances they are only generators of pain. A nail is driven out by going through the required mourning, respecting our sadness, analyzing our share of responsibility in the break-up that we have gone through, thinking on how can we be better the next time, and that we will keep a closer look to avoid suffering again in the same way. There are no shortcuts to achieve wellness; we cannot jump necessary stages.

You may even come across the right person for you, but if you haven't come out of the transition, you may lose the opportunity or you will incur mistakes that will scare that person away. Remember that if you did not fill the hole left on the wall, it doesn't matter if you paint the wall of the prettiest color you can find, you will always see the defect, and for those who come near you, it will be unavoidable to notice this empty space, as well as your lack of carefulness for not filling it.

Irrational beliefs related with the children

-My friend, I really believe that I am going to look for a way to get pregnant and thus keep him from leaving me. As soon as we have a baby, the relation will improve.

Probably the saddest part here would be to think that you need somebody else to keep your partner from leaving you. That you had to take advantage of an innocent being who has no responsibility of the erroneous way of loving that you learned. A son brings a very heavy load into our lives. Those of us who are parents like to repeat that a son is the most beautiful thing in the world, that he is the best thing that has ever happened to us, that it represents a life mission. But when you have been sleepless for three months because the baby wakes up every two or three hours, the perception changes and we know that not everything is marvelous.

People who believe that a son can tie down a man or a woman, are irrational. Maybe it will do it physically, but that person is not going to love you well, he will mistreat you and the son is going to resent this. He is going to know that you used him. Many times, this happens when a man wants a woman to get pregnant to keep her from growing, to stay at home all the time, to keep her from surging. And in the end, we will only have two empty and sad beings, tied by the same fear of being alone or to start again.

I spoke with a woman in her forties who had a twelve years old daughter from her first relationship.

At the moment I met her, she had just ended a two-year relationship and she had found out that week that her ex-boyfriend was already going out with another woman and that he looked very happy. The reason she came to my practice was that she couldn't take out of her head the temptation to call him, seduce him and try to get pregnant by going out with him a few times and by these means making him come back. She was convinced that this man was a good father, and that if she gave him a son, he could not leave her. During the session, through adequate questioning, I confronted her with that plan: ¿do you want him to come back for you or for the son you are going to have? ¿If you love him so much, how come you don't respect him? ¿On a scale of 1 to 100, how much do you believe he will remain in a relationship like that? ¿How can you suppose that he will love you if you don't love yourself? ¿Why do you want him to come back if you know he doesn't love you and that he is happy with someone else?

She disappeared after that session and turned up again after eleven months. She had been able to carry out her plan. She looked for him, she found him, she seduced him and got pregnant; but he continued with his other relationship. Now she had two daughters from two different men and now had to face the fact that her method to find love did not work: she must understand that sons and daughters are not a chain for a lock and that to believe that a son" will make him stay", has failed twice. She had to accept that only now that she was suffering, she remembered our first session and all the questions I asked her; she also regretted not having simply given herself the opportunity to take a good look inside of her and change some beliefs. Unfortunately, in this instance as well as many others, those beliefs that we repeat as parrots from generation to generation and without thinking, have made her life more difficult and left another child with an absent father and a sad mother.

People who think that a son is going to fix a dysfunctional or ended couple relationship, are completely and absolutely irrational. A son is a very serious commitment that is going to deteriorate the relation of the couple if it is not a solid one. ¿How many people who have kids sleep more now, rest more or have more sex? At least during the next eighteen or twenty years of our lives we will be guiding them and dedicating a great part of our time and energy to raise them and care for them. So, put your feet on the ground and understand that if you didn't have a good method to keep you partner next to you; after having a son, you will not have a method, the time or the energy to do it. You'd better look for another option. If you don't want to do it for yourself, then at least do it for that being who is coming to an unstable home and that will repeat your story for sure. Our sons take up a lot of our energy because those of us who want to be good parents need to use a lot of our time to achieve it.

Irrational beliefs related to change

-If he really loves me, he is going to change everything I ask him to, he will stop having friends and is going to spend Sundays with me instead of going to the softball game.

-If she really loves me, she is going to let my children spend more time with my family, she is going to stop wearing tight clothes and she is going to stop chatting with her friends.

¿How many times have you started a relationship as a couple and only two weeks later you are asking your partner to change? Let's be honest: many of us have started a relationship with a person that is not the best version of what we want for us and we immediately start asking our partner to make changes. ¿Why do we do this? Why do we believe that love can solve everything, that if him or her loves me enough, him or her is going to change for me? Because we have heard so many times in soap operas and movies from princes and princesses that if someone loves you, this person will change for you.

In my professional practice I have seen many times how one of the partners has profound resentments towards the other because they feel obligated to make changes they don't want to, and when you do that, you generate a lot of anger inside of you; not only towards the person that forces you to change but also towards yourself, causing both unnecessary diseases and stress. Stop being what you are is never an option: we can improve certain aspects of our personality, but if you love softball or to go shopping with your friends, and your partner wants you to stop doing it, you will soon be enemies, even though you are sleeping in the same bed.

A girl sent me a message on my social networks saying:" I constantly complain to my partner asking him to stop chatting and exchanging sexual photos with other women; I have begged him to change that but he only answers me saying that that really does not affect me because he is not going to leave me for them; he says it is a good distraction for him. And here, even though it may sound a little senseless, it would be ideal for her to understand that he is happy doing that, and that also, he doesn't want to stop doing it and that he doesn't feel any motivation to change and that the most important thing is that he is not connected with her, he doesn't understand his pain or discomfort. In this case, it would be worthed to lose all hope at once and to accept that there is no possibility of change; that she has been begging for love and fidelity for a while and from somebody who doesn't want to give it to her.

The ideal situation is that both partners be complete with their life – I know that it sounds utopic, but it is possible- and once they both have a job, friends, pass times, family and a life of their own, then they can get together to make their life even better.

When I ask someone to change something that makes him happy, I am not loving him. I usually tell my patients: ¿if you love that person so much, why don't you let him go and allow him to find someone who can be a better match for him or her, but you don't do it? That is why couples who get separated and get back together again, are together all day long, but that wears out in a couple of weeks. The change that occurs after two weeks of separation is not real. I recommend my patients a minimum of six months to evaluate and determine if the partner is constant in the apparent change, and that it is a change out of his own initiative. Only after that you will be able to know that the change really occurred and that it isn't just the nostalgy of getting back together or for fear of being alone.

Irrational beliefs related to details:

-If that detail were for me, I would like it.

Or

-If you bring a detail, is because I told you to, and not because it comes from your heart.

Or

-You should know what I like because it is obvious, you already know me.

We have all been asked sometime to be fortune tellers or even worse, that we know it all. And all of us would like the other to know it all, that the other person knew exactly which are the foods and drinks that we like, the color and brand of the handbag we prefer, or to what place I want to go.

I remember a patient who arrived to my practice very upset: she was preparing her son's birthday and hated her husband because he did not know anything about materials and didn't help her to choose the table cloths for the party. She was so upset that she even considered cancelling the celebration. And believe me, I have a son and I have never taught him anything about materials. Imagine if we had to teach absolutely everything to our children in order for them to get in a relationship and be able to please their partner in every aspect. This doesn't happen in real life; we have possibly watched a lot of Hollywood movies that inspire magical thoughts. That has to do with the fact that we irrationally suppose that, if someone loves us, this person should know everything we like.

Almost all women who come to my practice – and this doesn't happen so much with men – they want a man who pays attention to details. And it just so happens that not everybody gets that kind of education at home. To pay attention to details can be learned as a habit, just as kids learn to brush their teeth. No doubt it is something that can be learned, but without expecting to be foretold. You will have to teach your partner what you like and what not.

An adolescent was telling me that she was very upset because she went out with a guy that according to her was perfect, sweet and handsome, but that everything turned out not "perfect" for her because he did not open the car door for her. The guy is seventeen years old and it is his first car, but she expected him to be immediately virile, polite, and that he "knew" that such detail was a must in order to make a woman happy. I had to show her that maybe nobody taught him how much it means for a woman that someone opens the car door for her. Maybe he has a father who doesn't pay attention to details or that he is the first person with a car in that family. There are thousands of reasons that could explain why he didn't open the door for her, and the fact that he didn't do it doesn't make him imperfect. The opening of a car door is done by a human being that was taught to do so. When I asked her if she had told the young man that she would have liked him to get the door for her, she said: "he should know we all like it". This is how we are; we seem to come from the factory like this, with strict and rigid beliefs that we expect our partners to know and that they carry out all of our fantasies and on top of all that, that I don't have to show them how I like to be loved.

Irrational beliefs related to Fidelity and Infidelity

-¿Doctor, after how many years of marriage is it normal to have an unfaithful partner?

The fact that this question exists in some people's mind means that "infidelities" are normal and that we only have to hope that they occur at the right time. Never assume that it is normal for your partner to be unfaithful to you.

Probably, the person who asked this, grew up watching a parent tolerating infidelity, and that may be the reason the person wants to know when it is the least painful, "because normal it already is". An infidelity will always be the consequence of a bad relationship; in some areas both were careless and allowed a third person to enter. Anyone who tells you that was unfaithful to you, even though this person loves you and that the relation is good, is lying to you. Infidelity = unhappiness in the relationship.

Another subject seems to be "if my partner is unfaithful to me at the right moment, then he or she should be forgiven". An infidelity is not forgiven. It is accepted or it is not accepted. And you work as a couple to seal the circumstances that led to the infidelity. Stop talking about forgiveness as something that him or her has to gain with sacrifice. Where there is humiliation, sacrifice or begging, there is no love, but rather a desire for power and control. And where there are or have been infidelities, there are things that need to be fixed on both sides.

Many people come to therapy sessions with a clear idea of what is causing them pain and what they could do to change it, but they pretend like they do not know it. They get distracted talking about the "guilty" person of causing their disgrace, of their long stories as a victim, of the responsibility that their parents have for what is happening at the present time.

And I know that if many of them had the courage to see the present and the pain they endure, they would be able to achieve wellness much faster. The price of not feeling is not to be able to see the truth and you pay dearly for that. "Pain is the price you pay to endure" says the psychologist and writer Phil McGraw.

Every time that you have an automatic thought, it comes associated to an emotion, whether it be fear, anger, happiness or sadness. That emotion fixes that thought and becomes a belief. We all walk around the world with the burden of our beliefs expecting and wanting them to be true and that is why they are irrational. Every time you have a belief that generates pain, ask yourself this question: ¿does this occur in 100 percent of the cases, every time and always? If the answer is yes, then we must be talking about a law, like the law of gravity or like the fact that all babies are born in a maximum of nine months. If the answer is no, then we are talking about a belief that is "yours" and that you have acquired from your caretakers throughout your life.

Most of the people who come to my practice, come in convinced that their belief is a true one, that they are right; that is why they convert it into a law and therefore the wrong is on the other person.

A law and a belief are not the same. The Law of Gravity applies here and in Shanghai. It is a law that can be verified in all of the planet. But the beliefs of people do not apply to all people and under all circumstances. When we say "the man I find will have to support me ", we are turning a belief into a law. And those who live their lives based on that "law", do not experiment how good it feels to the women who invite the man to go out, pay for the check, and take control.

Let us stop repeating obsolete, absurd and false beliefs. We can start working on our beliefs so that they do not become laws, to avoid repeating the things we have learned and that lead us to be unhappy and to make unhappy the people around us. The only way to change is to take a look at our beliefs. Don't stay with what you know; don't accept or hang on to irrational beliefs that you may have about love, because if you don't, you will not be able to move forward with this thing about being a better partner.

The beliefs that set us on wrong paths

I suggest you do this exercise:

Close your eyes and locate yourself in those situations that you have incurred in a couple relationship that didn't work. Think about how much and how many times this person has shouted to you and then always apologized repeatedly. Think when and who has assaulted you, even physically, and afterwards has told you "I love you, I am sorry". Think when and who has hung up on you once and again making you feel useless and invisible. Remember if someone has cheated on you repeatedly with lovers, if he has made fun of you in front of other people and also during moments of intimacy. Think on the face of that person, what he said, how he looked at you. Think about why, how and how far did you follow that person that hurt you and that knew what he/she was doing. Remember who and when has hurt you and has made you believe it was your fault. If you have lived and felt all of this, then you know what a toxic love is. Many of us who have been involved is a relationship as a couple, have sometime been immerse in a toxic love. I would even go as far as taking the word "love" out, but we wouldn't know how to define it. Every time I ask in my practice: "why are you here"? the answers I get are "because he hits me", "because he hurts me", "because he has another woman with children", "because he mocks me constantly", etc., I then ask: "what are you waiting for"? And they say they are not waiting for anything and they also add: "I love him" or "I love her". Many believe that that is sufficient reason to stay in a relationship as a partner. And you know what? It is not!

I always try to get my patients ask themselves "why am I in this relationship", instead of simply asking "why". This is a powerful question that helps to clarify the original fantasy that love can solve everything. The answer is not easy and sometimes it takes several minutes. Sometimes there isn't a "what for"? Those who live in situations such as these, unless they have a disorder beyond the psychological area, they have a bad love or a sick love. It is not possible to love someone who hurts us; this is incongruent. This is not love. Maybe you feel at ease with that, maybe it is what you have learned, maybe you are "comfortable" with that; but it is not love. It must be said out loud to ourselves and others: that is not love.

¿Why do we bare what is unbearable"? Everything in life has to do with our beliefs. The behavioral-cognitive trend that I learned to work with after graduating as a psychologist, reaches deep in the thoughts of people assuming that the irrational or dysfunctional thought patterns cause an equally irrational behavior – that brings with it undesirable consequences- and negative emotions. We look for the center of these thoughts to heal them, because we know that those thoughts are based on beliefs. I am aware that this can be a confusing, however, it is vital that it is understood, because it is the essence of the method that I suggest so that "I can be a good partner".

I have heard irrational beliefs of all kinds, just like the ones mentioned in previous pages, however, I would like you to take a paper and pencil and start answering the following questions:

¿What do you believe about love"?

¿According to your parameters, what do you think is correct and incorrect when you are a partner as a couple? What do you think about hurting and infidelities? Are there situations in which you justify these conducts.?

¿What did your parents tell you about how to respect your partner"?

¿How could you tell that they loved each other"?

¿Who is the weak part and who is the strong part of the relationship when you have a partner?

Throughout this book, this information can help you move forward more quickly before the changes you want to make.

Every time a person sits in front of me asking for help, I start by explaining that psychological health consists of a "think-feel-do" in a straight line. It is to say that if I THINK(1) that I will become the next Miss Venezuela, I think of the dresses I will have and in my runways?, then I FEEL (2) great happiness and I feel proud and want to jump of joy when I think about the crown, and I ACT (3) taking care of me, watching my diet, working out and improving every day in order to win. Here I would be thinking, feeling and acting in a straight line. ¿Yes or not? And here is where many people fail to reach this straight line, because even though they think and feel with coherence, they still act irrationally.

Imagine this Miss to be, that after thinking and feeling correctly, ACTS (3) eating junk food at all times and continuously gaining weight. There would be an incongruency between thinking, feeling and acting, which will in turn and without a doubt would make her lose and suffer.

I am going to give another example in line with the subject of the partner. A patient that came to my practice in Caracas used to tell me: "I think I must go back to my job because I liked it very much and when I do it I FEEL(2) happy and productive; besides my fear of dependency disappears, but I ACT(3) staying at home so that my husband doesn't get upset; he is very jealous and believes it is not healthy for me to go out to work." You see? Incongruence between thinking, feeling and acting. Which will lead my patient as well as the Miss to be, to lose and suffer. This is the first analysis you must do about your beliefs and behaviors, one by one. Take the time you need, because this will give you self-recognition, which is the best tool for a life with well-being.

In general, we get along just fine, we get into relationships or we talk to people that have our same combination. I generally feel like a fish in the water with those people that speak just like me and that see life the same way I do. That is why we see groups of toxic girlfriends together, having a cup of coffee and repeating "screw him, be unfaithful to him, do the same to him, don't mind, don't give him sex for a week".

Why? Because they like to keep in company with their equals. Misery loves misery as company. By the same token, we see people who are successful and productive in groups and we usually say that "money calls more money". But this is not true. The reality indicates that we get easily related to people who are similar to us and think the way we do.

The other day I was speaking with a friend who had stopped going out with her cousin - who had a terrible relationship with an abusive husband - because it irritated her cousin to hear how well her marriage was going and how happy she was. They somehow went their separate ways because they did not share neither the same misery nor the same happiness. This is a formula that normally works out. See who you relate with, who are those four or five persons that you see more frequently and you will notice that you have the same beliefs and a "similar" life to those of the other group.

Therefore, in order for ME to be a good partner I must revise my beliefs concerning love and my partner; to evaluate if they are rational, to work in order to establish congruence in my thoughts, feelings and actions, and besides, to carefully choose who do I share my time with.

Appendix 1:

Revising my beliefs.? Which of the previously described beliefs guide my life today? __________

____

¿How do I describe myself when I am with my partner? (consider all possible dimensions) _________

____

How have your partners described you? What do they say about your behavior as a partner? (consider all possible dimensions) ____________________

____

What are my strengths, weaknesses, opportunities and threats when I am in a relationship with my partner? ___________________________

____

Now that I have written all of this, I realize that ___

____

What is your most important need?

Every person we meet wants something, longs for something with all of his soul, that "something" that is "indispensable" for every individual. We all have needs, but somehow, we are all led by a different one. And at this point it becomes very important to know which is yours to help you find and keep a good partner.

If the most important thing for you in life is the search for certainty and control –and I mean the control over your own conduct, people around you, plans and circumstances– you need to know what is predictable and have an agenda, to know at what time you are going, at what time you will come back, how much do you make and how much do you spend. The control is the beacon that guides your life; if you can do things the way you have planned them, you will feel good. People who want to have stability, and certainty, could sometimes appear to be so focused and competitive in trying to achieve their objectives that they can easily be perceived as someone cold and indifferent. But no, they are only using their time and energy on the achievement because it gives them security and security gives them power and control. These people are very trustworthy and real entrepreneurs, but not too affectionate. ¿Why? Because the "perfect" achievement comes first. And to create warm and close relationships takes time that they are not ready to give up.

If the most important thing in your life is change, different things, to vary, to practice various sports, to have various groups of friends, different styles of clothing, and a variety in just about everything you can, then you will always be open and flexible for whatever comes up, you will not need an agenda because you know how to flow. You think it is marvelous that someone is able to change plans without complications and that such an event does not represent a chaos. To enjoy getting up early, but not to comply but because you want to make the most of each minute of the day in your multiple tasks and groups; it is not difficult for you to be noticed because of your fresh character, your good mood and even intelligence to handle groups and meetings. These persons are very much fun, vibrating and enriching, but not very trustworthy. Why? Because fun and flow come first. And they are neither going to negotiate nor are going to become predictable people who live by a previous agenda.

If you are a person for whom the most important thing in life are the relationships you develop with others – love, give and receive affection, avoid conflict at all cost, even above yourself- you will always place other people first, you will always try to make other people happy whatever it costs, or at least, make them feel comfortable. In many moments of your life, you will assume a submissive conduct so that you won't lose the people you love and the worst thing that could happen in your life is that somebody had a bad opinion about you. Most of the times you will estimate the value of a person based on how much of your time this person represents in your life and all the good memories you share. That is why it is so difficult for you to end a friendship, even when this friendship is not convenient for you. These people are usually loving and generous, but they are not honest, because keeping most people around them happy comes first and in some occasions, they will lie to themselves and to others just to maintain a perfect harmony.

If the most relevant thing in your life is to be important –your status, to be right, to know how things are done and have the world listen and respect you– you will have as your main job to study everything, to be documented, to make decisions with a rational and logical criteria in order to also convince those around you and gain the importance you need. If you belong to this group of people, success and achievement as well as the straight A's are not so important as to recognize that success. You are not oriented towards finishing that perfect task but rather to have people recognize you, get applauded for it and to issue good reviews and comments.

It is very common to feel attracted to people with our same emotional needs; we recognize each other in that point: it must be great for two persons who are hungry of control and certainty to be together; to imagine clear agendas, no surprises, concentrated plans, stable relationships with specific agreements, but… it could become a boring relationship, dry, mechanical and far too predictable. Just the same as for two persons addicted to variety and change, to be together would be like an explosion of passion, happiness, large amounts of endorphins, but… how would it be to have two irresponsible adolescents together and without rules: too unstable and non-predictable; and two lovers of love, to avoid conflict they would have an idyllic relationship, one of fantasy and permanent caring mimes, where both would have a tank full, but… extremely submissive, doing whatever is necessary to maintain that stability and linear affection. And finally, two lovers of important things who will the wonderful experience of having someone that applauds every action, they will feel glorious because of recognition and living with a person who knows how to do things right, but… too much perfection together with an extreme need of "tell me I am valuable". The ideal situation lies in loving someone who can be on our side to fill our needs, because that person can teach us something and be a complement for us. And here it is very important that you understand that we do have different needs and that we know that it would be ideal to be with people who have needs different from ours, we could be preparing a checklist for when we want to start looking for a partner or to improve an existing relationship.

For example, if the most important thing for me is control, when I am with a person for whom the most important thing is variety, I must allow him to satisfy that need. If I am with somebody and I know his need and I insist that he doesn't fulfill it, I am not being a good partner. ¿Do you recognize yourself as a person who wants to be in control? ¿Do you like to have your feet on the ground, to manage your agenda and finances? ¿Do you identify yourself as a person who likes to have fun and enjoy life? ¿Do you like the variety, change and are you one of those persons who likes to try all kind of different things in bed? ¿Do you identify yourself as a person who loves relationships, to have many friends, to do well unto others, and to avoid conflict at all cost? Is there an ethical person inside of you? Is it important for you to be important?

This need has to do with the way we learn to be loved since we are kids. A person who loves to be in control and to do perfect things, for example, learns to get love because of the things he does and does well-like when you hear about a kid "who is little and already writes well, adds and subtracts"; that kid tells himself "when I am perfect and I do things right I am in control of everything and people love me". When you have someone who needs variety in his life, you will hear him say that, since he was little, he used to play basketball, swimming, soccer, and he did it all very well, because he was changing all the time and he was very energetic. While those who love love and good relationships you will hear them say that they were children "so sweet, always giving kisses and hugging people, they intervened between kids who were going to fight, and shared everything they had.

"since those kids know that they are loved that way and that only by being that way they would receive love. And if you are one of those persons who loves to be a guide, being important and to do everything with high ethics, you would hear people describing you in your childhood as a child who became the man of the house, his mother's husband or the wife of her father, the child who everybody asks for advice and knows how to do it, or so it seems.

When we understand that no need is good or bad, that no one is better than another, and that that was the way we learned to be loved by children, we will stop judging ourselves and others. I cannot hurt someone else because he learned to gain love by being diversified or by being mimed. I can only respect our differences and learn from them. And if the other is a very aggressive combination for us, the ideal thing would be to end that relationship as a couple and to start looking for someone that complements us in a better way. To realize which is the most important human need brings us much closer to understand the other person from humbleness. The task of all human beings is to possess a little of those other needs that we are not anxious to fill.

I invite you to observe starting today with an open heart what you need and what does your partner need from the emotional point of view. I invite you to discover who you are and to learn about that boy or girl that still lives within you. It is necessary to accept that we are different.

How did I learn to express love? How do I know if I am being loved?

Two questions that are vital to any human being who wants to be a good partner. When we are growing, our parents show us with their actions how they express love, just as through life we learn being their sons which is their way of loving us. And that language that they use, we assume to be "normal" or "correct".

Later on, as adults, we go out into the world with our learned language and we look for our partners to show our love "just like we learned at home" and here we have another fundamental step in the process of ME being a good partner. You need to know in which language you express love. ¿Can you imagine if you only speak Spanish and tomorrow you meet your ideal partner but this person only speaks German? What would you do" Do you discard him immediately? ¿Do you start teaching him Spanish? ¿Do you start learning German? ¿Do you get upset and you insult him because he didn't learn Spanish?

The ideal situation would be that both made a commitment to learn each other's language, that way there would be justice and equality and they would show each other how their "language of love" works. If I fall in love with someone that expresses love in a different way that I do, I begin to "think and feel" that he is not loving me or that he is doing it wrong. And immediately start appearing irrational beliefs, those that make us suffer and lose. "If he or she loved me, he or she would do this or that", as if he or she had to guess his or her language.

Throughout my career as a therapist, I have seen people who love in different languages of love, that I also call "channels" or "ways". Some authors have talked about this in the past. I talk about what I have seen in my professional practice and I must clarify that I have also seen who never learned how to express love, simply because he or she never received it.

> **Words:** There are lovers who express what they feel by constantly talking. They say "I like you", "I love you" and they give each other sweet nick names to express affection. They say phrases like "my baby", "my pumpkin", "honey", "my life", "how beautiful you are", "how handsome you look", "how intelligent

you are". They leave notes on the refrigerator doors, they place a post it in the rear-view mirror of the car, love letters. In summary, words, words, words.

Gifts: There are people who use material things to prove their affection since they put their best love intention in material things. They choose carefully that thing that they feel will make you happy. They will meticulously choose the color, fragrance, and even the shape that will draw your best smile; they will never buy anything without thinking it over very well since these lovers express their love "selecting the best gift for you".

Service: There are people who express their love giving presents even doing nothing. They go straight home from work, they are always early for whatever appointment they may have, they sit next to you while you are reading, cooking or watching TV. They are there with you. These people express their love by "being present".

Physical Contact: There are people for whom touching you is the best expression of their love, they make all possible efforts for you to feel physically close to them while you are there with kisses, hugs, with their leg on top of yours, touching your hair, rubbing their hands against yours. These people love by "touching".

I remember a couple that came to my practice where she complained with great grief that he never told her that he loved her, that he was dry and even assured that the problem was his "sick" family because nobody expressed love.

And when I turn around towards him to ask him for his point of view regarding his wife's opinion, with a confused and embarrassed face he said: "I am always buying her things that make her happy; I choose carefully and plenty ahead of time everything I know she likes and she always gets a bouquet of roses on a Friday night". He was loving her with gifts and all she wanted were words. It is something similar to a bar code reader that did not codify the roses nor the details. For her, he was not loving her because he never said it. On his side of the story, he felt very frustrated and claimed that she was an endless pit since, no matter how hard he tried, he could never get her to thank him for any of his presents. He also thought that she did not love him. You see? There are no errors nor mistaken people and certainly no bad intentions; what we have here are kids from different homes that love in a different language, and neither one of the two, up to that moment, had been humble and brave enough -something they would later learn in therapy - to accept that they only needed to learn each other's language.

Why do we love in a certain way? Because we learned it at home, it comes from our childhood, no matter who were the persons that raised us, they showed us how to express love. If I identify myself loving in a certain way and I find a partner who loves in a different way, the best way to handle the situation is to talk about it, to share the information, to define what is it that each one likes the best and to start loving your partner in a language that him or her can understand, as well as negotiating the same for you. It is fundamental for you to understand that it may take a while to each partner to learn the language of the other and perhaps a little more to learn to use it. Remember the Spanish-mandarin example. It is a new language and we need to be conscious of the commitment and time that it will require.

The important thing here is to know who you are, that you understand the language of love that you use and want to receive, and that the same is happening to your partner. It just may be to learn to be humble. It has to do with a language, a means of expression. There is no good and no bad, there are no wrong languages, they are all correct, only different. Perhaps the game of life is to learn to be humble about this.

What tendency helps me to be a good partner: ¿aggressive or submissive?

Ever since we were born, each and every one of us will have a specific temper, that is why there are crying babies, not quiet, that never sleep; but there are also quiet ones, peaceful and who sleep more than they need. Then we start to grow up and once again, observing our caretakers, we begin to learn how they react to different situations and we begin to shape our character based on what we learn. As adults we find people who have learned and chosen to be submissive and others aggressive. In my experience treating human suffering, I have seen that both attitudes produce discomfort.

In our Latin-American culture, we value it very much when a person doesn't allow anybody to step on us or put us down, to be careful and to permanently have a defensive attitude, especially in couples. The most common expression used by Latin-American grandmothers is: "make sure you study my dear because if the man turned out to be bad for you, you can kick his behind and throw him out." Or: "never give your wife the control of the house or the finances because they are very manipulative and leave you out on the street; it is best if you are in command."

Before these teachings, what we are observing at present… becomes obvious: millions of destroyed relationships, people that were supposed to be together to love each other now ended up hating each other. Why? Because nobody has taught us that the ideal situation is for us to be assertive. That is, do not choose to be a submissive person nor an aggressive one. Both end up having a bad life, with bad results.

How can we be assertive?

Step 1:

If I face an unpleasant situation where someone is hurting me, what is the right thing to do? To tell this person what I don t like or what is bothering me, to ask that person to do it differently, to show that person some different options, to talk it over or come to an agreement. Many persons avoid a conversation because they do not want to cause a fight or because they don't want their partner to be criticized, however, if this is not done, it only makes the situation worse, it generates resentments and strikes self-esteem. Finally, to silence the problem is the worst option; it may seem to be apparently easier, but certainly the worse.

It is highly important that you never use the word "you" when you are communicating with your partner about something that you do not like; the correct choice of words would be something like "I" or "I would like" or "I need" or "it would make me very happy". To use the word "you" during a negotiation is an error that raises a wall in the communication. It is not the same to say "you should get home earlier", than to say" I would like it if you got home earlier". The first one is an order and even a judgement. The second is a piece of information about me and what does me good.

Step 2:

If the situation repeats itself, we must remember what we have talked about: "do you remember what we spoke about that day and we agreed…" At this point it is very important to validate with the other person who knows what agreement I am talking about and, if possible, at all, to commit to it again. Sometimes, the first conversation or agreement established in the middle of an emotional crisis, with plenty of anger, sadness or even frustration; that is why the agreement wasn't completely clear for at least one on the two. That is why a second conversation, detailed and quiet, happens.

Step 3:

And if an unpleasant event should occur a third time, we are now facing the real fact that the other person simply is not listening or doesn't want to be with you. At this point we must face that in reality our method is not working and that we must change strategy. When an event happens a third time, is because the other person is not connected with you and doesn't understand what you need, or what causes you pain, and therefore you need to do something different. It is pure statistics.

There are patients, especially women, that have told me in my practice: "I have been repeating the same thing for three years, about what I don't like, and he keeps on doing it" or "I have been telling him what hurts me for two years and he doesn't change", or "she is always in a bad mood, the days go by and no matter how many times I say it, she doesn't improve". What do you expect" a miracle? Do you expect the extraterrestrials to come and exchange him for somebody else"? How can you repeat something for days or even years and you keep doing it without noticing that it doesn't work? How much time are you willing to waste? |

In general, we are not taught to be assertive and we do not know how to be assertive. Starting today, decide if you have to cry, complain, victimize yourself (submissive attitude), or if all to the contrary you have to insult, scream or chase away your partner from the house (aggressive attitude). Both perspectives are in the wrong place. The mid-point is the correct position, leave the science fiction for the movies if you have already said it a couple of times and your discomfort doesn't matter to him. Eliminate both options, aggressive and submissive, from your possible choices and move towards assertiveness.

To be desirable or lovable? What is better?

The world sells us the idea that we must be desirable. And in order for this to happen we are all supposed to have the same body style, to look the same as far as the fashion is concerned, use the same brands of clothes, to be a graduate from a recognized university, to live in only certain areas of the city and if at all possible, to have renown last names. However, only a little weight is given to being lovable, that means to learn to support your partner, to learn to listen, to be one with your partner's problems and happinesses, to learn to share money and responsibilities.

Those persons who only focus on being desirable, probably have someone always by them, good sex and groups of other attractive persons –in all possible ways– but it is very likely that those relationships are neither very deep nor lasting. They are surrounded by people, but they are alone. They cannot count unconditionally on anyone. Why? Because they only consider important what is on the outside, to the physical aspects, to that expression of "I have so much, I am worth so much". And from the outside it is difficult to make a connection from essence to essence with others.

I have heard expressions such as "he makes love to me every day and shows his desire for me at every moment, but he is incapable of telling me about his projects and plans"; "she is gorgeous and a goddess in bed, but she is no good when it comes to doing business; she must leave that to me, I cannot rely on her".

On the other hand, people who only focus on being lovable are very much appreciated, requested and sometimes even abused. This group believes that their appearance doesn't really matter, what is important is "how much does the other contribute", "how much can the other help". To be desirable is not vital for these people, by doing good unto others and that other people know that they are there is enough.

A patient told me once:" since I love him so much, I advised him to decide between his lover and I and not to extend this any longer, and I told him that I will always be there to help him think and make a decision". Well, No! Who are you" Mother Theresa? Are you some kind of therapist for your partner? Do you think you have to understand him in everything and to back him up in everything, even in his infidelities? No. But this is the damage of only wanting to be lovable, and at any cost. When we ask ourselves if it is better to be desirable or lovable, the answer is in the middle. If I am desirable to the other, that opens the door to sexuality and it is sexuality that makes us a couple, otherwise we would just be friends or business partners. This is about taking care of myself and to nurture myself both physically and intellectually, to attract my partner, to encourage variety and intimate games, to satisfy his desires and show him mine, and to maintain active the erotism each day of the relationship. She doesn't matter, it is always possible to nourish passion.

On the other hand, we stimulate our lovable essence. We are taught to be good with others, and afterwards, if there is anything left, good with ourselves. This is not right, because it generates a lack of equilibrium in a relationship. To be a good partner you need to love inwards and outwards. To be a good person with yourself and with others. This has to do with listening, listen to yourself, to support and to ask for support, to accompany and to enjoy companionship, to respect and be respected, everything in a two-way street.

You must create a deep friendship relationship with your partner, where each one wants and promotes and wishes the best for the other as well as for himself. You must make a commitment with yourself to live with the consequence of being desirable and lovable both to yourself and to your partner, and do not expect to receive any less.

What tendency will help me gain love: ¿to be a genuine or false person?

Throughout my professional practice, I have observed how the majority of my patients suffer because they live in some kind of confusion or dilemma when they have to choose between being absolutely genuine, transparent and honest with their partners, or on the contrary, always hide behind a mask created by them, with attitudes and actions that are "socially accepted" even though they are false and not internally true.

Most people choose the second alternative; he lives protecting himself of the opinions of other people, he wants to look well at whatever the cost, they get mimetized with every person or group they socialize with, and this brings as a consequence that sometimes the same person behaves in different ways, depending on who that person is with at the time.

What do false people look for? Acceptance.

Do they do it to harm others? No. They do it to protect themselves from other people not loving them.

Why do they use that method? Because they were sons of excessively criticizing parents, who compared them all the time with other people; parents who repeated to them every day how badly they did things, because they did not receive unconditional love and who believe that they must always pay for everybody's affection by "pretending to be perfect and adequate for the group".

It is normally understood that who is genuine is good and who is false is bad. The truth is that there are no such categories; what exists is what generates well-being and what generates discomfort. And being false generates too much social anxiety; anxiety to be found out, fear that people could know the real "ME" of the false we are referring to here.

I have heard some phrases that some parents repeated to persons with a tendency to being false, like for example: "your brother is better", "I don't know why I had you, you were a mistake in my life", "you will never be good for anything", "no one will ever want to live with you, no matter what you do, you will always end up doing something wrong".

A child who learned to live between criticism and shame will eventually end up thinking that he is not valuable enough, he will become false, he knows that if he shows himself as he really is, the rest of the world will not love him. They are not bad people; they are merely defending themselves; they are doing what they learned when they were little: to pretend, so that nobody notices how badly built they are, because that is what their parents have made them believe.

The complete opposite happens with genuine people; they were accepted children, they were told "you are not the best, you don't get the highest grades but I love you anyway", or "I am punishing you because you did something wrong but I love you just the same. You are valuable". This reinforces their value internally, whether they do things perfectly or not. People who are successful, happy and have a good couple relationship are generally genuine persons without fear of failing or making a mistake; they are not afraid to say "I don't know" or to ask for help. You can recognize them because they are expressive and honest, they are not afraid to show their weaknesses and even less their strengths, they don't suffer from false modesty and above all, they don't mind being wrong. They feel comfortable with what they have become and want to share it with others. It is generally very pleasant to talk with them because they will not try to sell you their point of view nor will make you feel guilty if you don't share it. Finally, they know that the fact that you aren't in agreement with them about something, has nothing to do with the love you feel for them; that is why they will not get away from you.

Many times, I hear from "false" people in therapy say things like "he is bad, he is good for nothing, but if I leave him and I don't find anyone else, I don't want to be alone". And here we see the tendency of "it doesn't matter if I am not happy but I am going to pretend I am", when the real truth is that it doesn't matter if you don't find anyone else, which is quite unlikely, but this is what these people think. The issue has to do with the fact that the person who is with you is not accompanying you, he is not doing any good to you and makes you feel lonely.

If you had to choose between being a genuine person or a false one, -and let it be clear that this has only to do with us and has nothing to do with anyone else-, the important thing is to check if you are afraid of not being sufficient and later you rewind the movie of your life to check the history of your family. And as it happens in most cases, it will not be true, we are all born with infinite possibilities, and then you say to yourself: "this belief is not mine, I was not born defective, my mother and father made me believe it but I have been able to achieve this and that. "This is because we all have achieved powerful things, good, positive things that have an impact. Look into it, you will surely find them. And if you still haven't achieved them, every day represents an occasion to do it, but it is fundamental that you choose not to live in shame and don't think of yourself as "barely capable".

Another example of the tendency to be a "false" person is to pretend being who we are not. Many women ask me in my practice: ¿and if I say that I love him and he feels excessively sure? And many men say:" the problem is that if I give her the control of the house and the money, isn't she going to want to control me? What does this tell us? That they enter a relationship with a pre-disposition, watching out for the other and placing barriers. And who builds barriers? Those who feel vulnerable and want to shield themselves. In reality, since life is uncertain, we don't know what things could happen or not, however, if they ever happened, if her boyfriend felt too sure or the wife of the other partner controlled him, well they would simply go their separate ways. Period. Nothing ties you to a person; only those childhood beliefs that made it clear to these children –todays adults– that always, no matter what they do, things will never turn out well. I believe that if I had to choose a single point as the most important of the method, it would definitely be this one, because understanding the gain in becoming genuine and accepting vulnerability as a part of life, will make the difference between living in hell or paradise. It is about understanding that we are human beings and that we are here to learn something every day and that this will require humbleness, will to learn, capacity to understand that there are other persons who have already walked this trail and that can provide knowledge, and above all, that it is alright to be afraid of the unknown. To understand that I am not weak because I get scared, that it is normal and just a part of life, that to avoid what causes you fear will allow it to grow until making your life miserable. One of the most vulnerable moments in life –the reason for which 70% of my patients come to my practice– are the separations. To get a divorce or a separation after several years of marriage is for many people a jump into emptiness. That is why we feel fear, anxiety, the postponing something for after Christmas, for after the birthday. We know that a divorce is neither easy nor comfortable; to jump to the unknown will generate a big fear in the stomach of uncertainty. But we shouldn't feel weak because of that since we are human beings and it is natural to sometimes being too attached to the presence –sometimes harmful– of our partner.

Most of my patients come to my practice looking for a magic recipe that will enable them to exit a relationship that makes them unhappy, quickly and without one drop of suffering." I want to leave him but I know I am going to miss him and that scares me", they tell me. What they really want is mental anesthesia. A vast portion of the planet is medicated, roaming around like zombies full of anxiolytics, antidepressives and sleeping pills. What for? So that they do not feel anything. So that it goes away very quickly. So that it doesn't hurt. Many even withstand horrible abuses to avoid the suffering after the breaking up. As Elizabeth Gilbert says in her book To Eat, To Pray, To Love, "we deserve something better than being together because of fear of being destroyed if we are separated".

For everybody –both genuine and false– to get over the sensation of a jump into emptiness is a real challenge, however, genuine people choose to leave a bad relationship without feeling like losers, they keep in their heads the reasons why they made the decision to get a divorce and at the same time they are clear that it doesn't represent a reason for being "worth less". They remind themselves every day that they love themselves and that they want the best for themselves. To stay in an agonizing relationship always implies the risk that one of the two -the most mentally healthy one- stops playing without previous warning. And this is what the false person doesn't foresee because of fear and that the genuine doesn't expect by emotional intelligence. There lies the difference between the two styles.

To be released from an unhappy couple relationship is a challenge to being constant, to bravery and courage, to clarity and detachment. You need to be conscious of your value and of what you deserve, then allow yourself to feel the sadness, the anger, the fear and cry as much as necessary; this is the only method I know to start building a healthy mourning with which you will become stronger and stronger as the days go by, until you reach the stage of acceptance, resignation and resignification, thus finding a balance between what you have learned and what was lost in the relationship; remember that being happy is a decision, it doesn't depend on the things that happen to us, but rather on the attitude we assume before the things that happen to us.

We cannot be afraid of living. If we do not show love, how can we expect the other to show it towards us? Why do we have to suppose that if I am a dry tree, he has to be sweet with me? The good love is a two-way street just like good sex and good communication. We are all afraid, many things make us feel vulnerable. We must assume that as something natural and ask us what is the worst thing that can happen? This is the most powerful question that I know. Do the exercise, start with a situation that causes you a great fear and go all the way to the end. For example:

–I want to talk with her with the same attitude she has towards me and that I don't like.

–And why don't you do it?

–I am afraid of her reaction, she always gets altered, the conversation gets worse, I don't get anywhere and at the same time I make the situation worse.

–What do you think is the worst that could happen?

–That she shouts, insults me and leaves.

–And if she shouts, insults you and leaves, what is the worst that could happen after that?

–Well, she may not talk to me for a few days.

–And if she doesn't talk to you for a few days, what is the worst that could happen?

–I don't know; that she may not want to get back with me and she may even find another man.

–And if she doesn't want to go back to you and finds another man, what is the worst thing that could happen? Which would be the worst consequence? Go all the way to the end.

–That I suffer, that it might hurt me to lose her and that we won't be together anymore.

–And if you suffer and it hurts you, and besides you are not together anymore, what is the worst thing that could happen?

–Well, nothing. Maybe I will suffer for a while and that maybe I won't find anybody else in my life.

–Even though it is quite unlikely that in a planet with seven billion people you will not find another person in your life, if you suffer and that really happens to you, ¿what is the worst thing that can happen to you? Dramatize, go to the worst scenario. What would it be?

–Well, nothing. That life goes on and that is all… Maybe I am really exaggerating.

And thus, you have just read how a cognitive-behavioral therapy session works in order to get to the bottom of how of the belief that produces fear. The ideal situation is to assume that we are human beings, that we don't have the answers to everything, that if we do something and make a mistake, we will look into it one thousand times to find the correct way to do it until we find it. This is the essence of being genuine: to work everything that can lead us to become false. And this way you will, for sure, get to be the best version of you as a partner because you will deserve a complete and genuine person.

Distrust, when we believe that to look out is to love

The top rule of love f or everyone who wants to be happy is to remember that we don't need to be martyrs by entering or remaining in a relationship with mistrusting, angry people who take a defensive attitude or who have traumatic unresolved life stories. The success of a relationship is measured by how much you give is how much you receive; this doesn't have to be millimetrically precise but fairly balanced. I am sure that throughout your life you have met people who seemed to have a special gift to take away their energy to those people that develop a relationship of affection; people who take the worst from others and that most of the time leave them with a sensation of exhausting emptiness.

To those who take extreme care for their things, to whom they constantly asphyxiate with doubts and reproaches, we must consider them as paranoid, jealous, vigilant, untrustworthy; that is, people who love making their partners feel guilty of something or that they are about ready to be so. For these lovers always on the lookout, it doesn't matter how well you behave or how many demonstrations of affection you give them: they will always look for and finding evidence that you are not as good as you want to make them believe and will always see your actions with a second intention. Today, many of my patients who love this way will check their partner's cellphones, bags, wallets, jackets, cars, e-mails, –they even follow them without being seen and even hire detectives– just to confirm their basic hypothesis that "I am sleeping with the enemy and if I don't keep my eye on the ball he or she will take advantage of me."

What is the fear behind this conduct? What motivates these people to constantly and uselessly protect themselves from their partners? Where does this unfounded fear come from?

Psychology establishes a series of correlations between the children we were and the adults we are. Cognitive-behavioral psychological investigations suggest that paranoid adults were children who lived in a constant uncertainty, where they could have suffered physical, sexual or emotional damages; children who surely grew in chaotic homes where the abuse, vices, being abandoned and criticized, were a constant. If a child lived in this sort of "war", it is absolutely normal that he learned to be always on the lookout and attentive before any situation and that due to his innocence he couldn't discriminate which one was dangerous and which was not; that is why he extrapolated it and decided to do it at all times so that he would be always protected. Not trusting anything or anybody is their most rooted belief.

In love and falling in love we can lower our defenses, allow someone else to come into our territory and to trust that person, otherwise the partner becomes a very difficult task for the paranoid lover, since in most cases they will not rest until they prove their cheating hypothesis or to make their terrified and diminished partners give in to telling them what they want to hear.

What should you do if you find yourself in a relationship of this kind? If it is you who is searching, following and looking into everything, allow yourself to get professional help; many of these symptoms and anxieties can be reduced by just learning to revise your thoughts and detecting which belong to your present reality and which do not. You will have the opportunity of getting to know yourself and to make peace with the child you were and that simply learned to be on the lookout all the time and at the same time you will be able to live a healthy love in which you will not be your partner's jailer, besides understanding that, not trusting, is the fastest way to be abandoned or to be lied to because you generate discomfort in the other person.

If it is your partner who is playing to be the jailer, then you have two options: the first and healthier one, to realize that loving is not to answer an interrogatory nor justify everything every day and at every moment; that you are not guilty of anything and that if you love your partner you can suggest getting help so that the relationship is not damaged beyond the point of no return and to understand that if he or she is not willing to, then it is time to leave. The second option is to stay and justify everything, answer to everything and lowering your self-esteem to minimum levels, to verify that you have done nothing wrong every time your partner asks you to do something, to go out only seldom or never, not have any friends, call in several times a day, learn to handle his/her anxiety crisis several times a day and to clarify everything as much as possible so that you don't raise any suspicious doubts.

Look for, not find

To "look for a partner" seems to be the most rejected expression on the planet. The expression "I am going to find me a partner right away" defines me as a lonely person, in need of affection, old, someone like Cinderella' s step sister and not the princess, because they are found by princes. And it is precisely this kind of fantasy-like education that has invaded a large percentage of the population choosing the option of loneliness. It is something like "before giving the appearance of someone desperate and having to show that I am looking for a partner, I convince myself that I am better alone". Or, "that is too much trouble and I don't want complications". The time goes by and every day more and more people leave this world without having experimented the wonderful experience of falling in love. In my years of professional practice, I have seen, with great concern, that many people still do not understand that the fact that we are looking for our partner among a countless number of potential candidates, is a personal, careful, thought and guilt-free task. Let's take a look at the definition given by different dictionaries for the term "look for":

Dictionary of the Royal Spanish Academy:

1. To do something to locate someone or something. I am looking for a book.

2. To do whatever is necessary to get something. Looking for work.

3. Said of a person. To do whatever is necessary so that something happens. You have asked for it.

ABC Definition:

It is known as the term of looking for that activity whose main characteristic is the purpose of the discovery of something.

Larousse Dictionary:

1. To try to find, get or discover a person or thing. Example: to look for an original gift.

2. Colloquial provocation, incite somebody. Example: Don't look for me or you will end up badly.

It must be pointed out that the words that are used to describe the "looking for" process like purpose, discover, do something, do whatever is necessary, to get, so that it happens. All of the words that locate us in an active, responsible, adult, engaging position, that we are capable of, that we know what and how we want it. I use and recommend using the expression" look for" because in order to do it correctly, first you had to know yourself what works and what doesn't in your life, what matches you, what makes you grow and what will diminish you. "To look for" is a process that starts by knowing what we are looking for and that is what makes it valuable. Instead, the word loved by our culture, the poems and songs, is "to find" and let' s look at what the DRAE (Dictionary of the Royal Spanish Academy) says:

1. To locate someone or something we are looking for.

2. To locate someone or something without looking for it.

3. Said by a person: to stump with someone else

4. To oppose someone, to antagonize with him.

We could even analyze that the origin of that word goes in an opposite direction to love. To find, to encounter comes from the Latin "in contra" threat is, opposite to.

Based on these definitions, it would mean then that in order to find something I must first look for something. Do you see it?

To find is a passive process by which you can run into something you are not looking for, that doesn't fit, that it is not what you are dreaming of, that it is not what will accompany you to create the best version of you. Let go the idea of "it is sad to be looking for a partner" and change it for "I know myself" I know what I want and that is why I am ready to look for a partner", in other words, "I got ready for this, it is a personal project, and I will do it the best I can, with all possible knowledge".

One of the most common questions I hear both in my practice as well as outside, is:" Doctor, what happens if we do not run into that person that we so much long for?". The point is not what happens but rather what are you going to do about it? To run into someone is not the required action. It is to coincide, to connect. It is to recognize each other as two persons who share values, interests and essences. Grasp this. This is your task because it is your life and your emotions that you are sharing with this person you choose. Don't go through life with that wandering soap opera about stumbling into someone; go through life with a giant magnifying glass looking for that something special which you already know is for you.

But what is to be done if you do not coincide with that person? The answer is actually very simple: keep looking for the next person, and the next and the next, until you find the one that looks like what you are looking for. But don't ever stop. Falling in love is so much worth your while that the search will never be in vain. I repeat: I am not saying "to find" because I believe it is irresponsible to assume that another person is like a bill that one can find as you walk on the street. The expression "look for" makes us more active and responsible. To look for and to find partners is another one of those false beliefs that we have been taught. We are told it is a process that happens by itself:" I am waiting for the right person to turn up for me", or "what is for me, will turn up by itself". To look for in order to find a partner has to do with a different method.

What is the first thing we need to do to look for a partner and falling in love afterwards? Create our model of a lovable woman or man will be a model created for you. The one that fits better with that which you want to live. When we are looking for a partner, we must know that everything that is external is going to wear off: beauty, teeth, hair and even the way we dress. We go through life looking for partners that are some kind of model.

Let's start; it is necessary to write things down –yes, with a pencil and a piece of paper– what is the most important thing for you in a man or a woman. You need to be very clear upon the values you look for in a person, his or her qualities, how does this person enjoy life, hobbies, occupations, family type and religion. Be as specific as possible, do not leave important details out. That list is a valuable possession for any healthy adult. What do you want in that partner you are looking for? You can write one million of "I want's". Don't feel like some things are dumb, useless or too picky. Let yourself flow. Write down everything that is important; it is your list and you can write down all of your desires. Do not allow other people to express opinions about your list saying things like "not this", "take this out", "this is stupid", "you should add that". It is a gift from you to you, so, give it your best shot.

Something I want to leave you in this chapter is my belief, based on my professional experience that a good couple is formed by two people who are very alike in essential matters. That is why is so important that what you are looking for isn't so different from you, especially in those things that make you happy. If you love the beach, it would be ideal that your partner did too, isn't it? If you are a faithful believer in your religion, wouldn't it be marvelous that your partner believed in the same things? It must be noted that I don't establish this as an order, but it would definitely be "ideal". It is not healthy to enter in someone's life thinking that we can change even this person's pass times and hobbies, and to think that if that person loves you, that person will change for you. To come to agreements with a person that is very different from you, many times generates stress. If everything that I want to do, whether it is eating or going for a ride, requires a negotiation, the relationship will become boring; you cannot enjoy anything if you are all the time negotiating and agreeing, negotiating and agreeing. Let' s be clear. We are what we are. Our nature will surface and that is why it is so important that we are with a person that is not too different from us in order to form a good couple. If you are in a couple and while reading these pages you realize that there are great differences between you two, then having the humbleness to accept it implies having travelled half of the road. What is this good for? Well, to check if there are points of convergence where we can find mutual support; or to allow us to get away from that person and be happy. There are no other alternatives, because the third alternative is to live together until death does its job, but this is not quite the best choice. We do not live here to donate our life to the selected suffering.

The "non – negotiables"

Once again, take a piece of paper and a pencil. Keep them in your hand bag, in your car, take them to meetings, to work, this is a very important task in order to become a good partner. Do you remember that a while back you wrote all the things you wanted in a man or a woman; ¿all of the things that would make you happy? Now let's proceed to the next step: from that list you made you will now select five things that you will not negotiate, in other words, you want them, period, those things that you know that without them you will not have the happiness you are looking for. Five things that will be your flag so that you will never fall for a situation, as we say in Venezuela, "catch whatever you can, it doesn't matter if it is very little".

What things are not negotiable? Everything that hurts us, everything that can cause us damage. One of my non-negotiables is that the man who lives with me must not have vices, and that includes cigarettes. To me, having to smell like a cigarette, is a form of aggression that I am not willing to negotiate. I always had breathing problems, I do not tolerate smoke, and on top of everything, my youngest son always suffered from asthma. I didn't want to live with someone who would be a walking chimney, not even if he were the most fascinating man in the world. Is this a foolishness? If I loved him would I accept it? If he were so perfect, how could I lose him due to something as simple as that? Could I make him quit the habit afterwards? If he loves me, he will quit it. ¡No! That does not work!

Even if he has the five thousand qualities of my list, if he smokes, this is a hello and goodbye. If I had to accept a man who smoked in order for me not to be alone – even though I know it would hurt me and my son – I would be planting the seeds of an inadequate relationship, because in the end it would become a test of powers and I would try to change him at whatever the cost to make him quit smoking and all this would do is to create resentment. The problem is not that he smokes. The problem is that I would negotiate something that I had declared non-negotiable, and everything just because of the fear of being alone.

In my time, I have heard an infinite number of non-negotiables. Here are just a few:

•That he/she has vices

•That he/she is not clean

•That he/she is bad in bed

•That he/she doesn't like children

•That he/she doesn't want to have children

•That he/she is unfaithful

•That he/she physically abuses me.

•That he/she has tattoos.

•That he/she makes friends too easily

•That he/she wants to see his parents every week

•That he/she wants to maintain a friendship with his ex.

•That he/she wants his parents to live with us.

•That he/she disappears and does not come to sleep at home

•That he/she has no initiative

•That he/she is a conformist

•That he/she has a religion different to mine

•That he/she wants to have pets

•That he/she doesn't pay attention to details

The "non-negotiables" need to be rational, they cannot go against what we want and need. We also cannot pass judgement upon our non-negotiables. It doesn't matter of other consider them dumb or silly, we must learn to respect ourselves, we must be genuine with what we like and what we don't like. The fact that people treat you with love and respect starts with the fact that you do it yourself; there is no other formula. Therefore, starting today, go out with your non-negotiables very clear and inside of you, and thus the probabilities of being wrong or suffering will decrease.

Observe yourself and evaluate if you are one of those persons who does not establish limits, that you do not know yourself, and therefore will negotiate everything, will accept everything, and suddenly find themselves alone or unhappy. If this is the case, it would be enough to check what makes you unhappy and that at the same time are hurting you just to have someone by your side. This is also another way to determine your "non-negotiables." To be always with our attention on what causes you pain and discomfort and that if you eliminated that from your day to day would produce a better version of you.

In one occasion, a patient was telling me that she wanted to break up with her boyfriend in spite of the fact that she loved him, and literally told me: "if he were taller and were willing to learn and work harder, I would stay with him". "¡In other words, he would be someone else!" Right? Here we could see that for her it was extremely important, besides, two items for her list of "non-negotiables": that he is shorter than her and that he is a conformist and has no initiative. You see now? The process is very simple and only requires a little practice. Pay attention to your own observations and flow with what turns up, write it on your list and then leave five red lights on and for which you will always come to a full stop and that you will know that you cannot proceed. Remember that if you run those red lights you may have an accident with very negative consequences.

The "where" is important, when we are looking for a partner

The place where we are going to look for a partner is vital. Looking for a good partner will be successful if we know at first where we could find him/her. The methods of searching will vary very much. What is fundamental is to be pro-active and active. We cannot expect that someone "arrives". This has to do once more with dignity. If I feel genuine, I can go and look for a partner whether in a Caffe, in a conference, at work, at the university or through social networks, anywhere, since that does not diminish me as a person. To admit that I want someone in my life is an act of absolute courage and intelligence.

You must meet people, go out to look for a partner with that objective, just like we have other objectives in life. Just as we say "I want to graduate" and we go to college for four or five years, just like when we want to find a job and we take our resume to ten companies, we look for a partner just the same.

We have been inculcated the taboo that going out to look for a partner is inappropriate. But it is not. We all deserve to live in someone's company, we deserve to have a person with whom to speak at the end of the day, someone to eat, go out and cry. We all deserve to make love the way we like it, we deserve to grow next to someone and not be judged for it. But if we don't go to the right place with a method to look for what we clearly deserve, it is likely that we won't find it.

What do people who are lonely normally say? Among other many things they say things like "I don't know anybody", "I don't have any friends who might introduce me to other persons", "I haven't been out in a long time". The invitation is for you to go out, to use the social networks, for you to get together with two or three friends in places where the people you are looking for could be.

You must think a little bit in order to find the right place. If I am looking for a man over forty years old, intelligent, with a position similar to mine, that likes to read the newspaper on Sundays and who enjoys some of the things I enjoy too, like studying or increasing my knowledge, an ideal place would be in a master's degree environment or the places where a certification of some kind is issued or an association that works with personal or professional growth. These are things I like. Each person has a model. Look for the places where that model that you have created when you made your lists of "what I want" and your "non-negotiables" hangs out.

Appendix 2

What characteristics are you looking for in a partner? ________________________________

____

____

____

What characteristics don't you want in a partner? __

____

____

____

Which of these characteristics that you don't like you are not willing to negotiate? (they must be 5, No more, No less) ____________________

____

____

____

That partner you have just designed with what you want and what you do not want, where could he/she be? Make a list ______________________________

____

____

____

What physical actions are you going to implement starting today to get near the objective of visiting those places and those potential partners? ________

____

____

____

Who are your allies in this project? Who would be your contention walls should you want to go back to your control area and not to go out to look for what you want? ______________________

____

____

____

When are you going to start? __________________

____

____

____

Men and Women are different. Can we accept it and love?

The feminine liberation, the metro-sexuality and other currents of thought of society tell us every day that men and women are equal, that we are the same, that we have the same rights, that we are equally successful, that we are made the same, but what they have forgotten is that we are biologically different – which has been more than proven – and that besides this has an impact in our conduct and our emotions.

They (women) are anecdotic and they (men) are forgetful

From seeing couples in my practice and through reading a very broad bibliography, it has become very clear that while women remember details from years past just as if they had happened a few hours ago, men sometimes have problems remembering why they had a fight with their partner yesterday. And this shows us the first big difference that it would be great to "accept". On the one hand men forget quickly and get rid of negative emotions and women store all the memories and maybe even classify them. Just like at the time of an ejaculation the man releases semen while women retain, take and keep the egg, during discussions men do not remember the details and let go while women can retain conflicts for years.

In my practice I have seen the astonished look of men when their partner tells the story of a fight they had at the beach sixteen years ago one morning when he was using a pair of blue shorts that they bought together in the shopping mall near their house. An excess of thoughts stored in a female brain to use them at the right moment.

The brains of men and women function in a different manner. It is biological and true, and there are scientific investigations that confirm it, even with images of MRI's where you can observe how, before the same situation, different parts of the brain are activated producing different conducts in each one. Those of us who are parents can see how much difference is there between a boy and a girl during their emotional and conductual growth.

The man, focused, not biologically prepared to handle all those tales of different times simultaneously, and also objective, had not understood anything, and only wanted me to summarize in a sentence what was happening with his sister. I understood and answered: “they broke up, they do not get along”. He nodded and said: “Okay”. That capacity to let go doesn’t allow men, in most cases, to hang on to long stories or exaggerated details. They easily get tired and saturated.

¿What to do?

Men: understand that your women need to talk, talk and talk, besides, every positive or negative detail will remain recorded somewhere in her mind to be used whenever necessary. That is why I always recommend to avoid unpleasant situations, since they will leave permanent memories.

Women: understand that your men will not remember details, not because they do not love you, but rather because their memory will be busy with the project or objective of that moment. To realize that we are different is a great tool to be the best version of ourselves as a partner and, as a whole, to wish us well.

Women are multi-focal and men are unifocal

That is why a woman retains so many things in her day to day life, many activities, she wants to do it all, work, take care of the kids, take them over, bring them back, cook. The man instead will only take care of what has been assigned to him or what he has assigned to himself, but he is not going to see what is everything that is required to get involved.

No one imposed upon women all the things that we do. Almost all things are imposed by ourselves, that is why at the end of the we may be exhausted, in a bad mood, feeling that life is unfair, but it is really our tendency and our desire to be needed what pushes us to do a thousand things at a time even though nobody has asked us. The man beside us has no idea of everything we have done, he doesn't care that things have been resolved, but not for the wrong reasons or because he doesn't care, but rather for mental savings, they are objective and it is difficult for them to spread out among non-essential activities. Thus, a woman cannot expect a man to act like a woman and a man cannot expect a woman to act like a man.

Women function on the basis of processes and sexual relations show it. For men it is a lot easier to have an erection and have sex a minute later. For us it is necessary that there be a preparation and a process. Our brain is biologically designed to function based on "steps". We could go back and see that at the beginning of mankind men were hunters who went out to catch food for their family and the woman would stay home to take care of the sons and daughters, she had to look after the children, she had to watch for animals that could attack, prepare food, do the chores of the cave, everything at once. The man only had to watch for what he had to hunt that day. One of the most frequent complaints of the women who come to my practice is that they, during the day at work, forget about them and that if by any chance they write a message it is short and cold. "I don't understand what is happening, Doctor, he leaves home at seven o'clock in the morning, not a call, it is like he forgot I was alive", they say. And Yes, that's how it is. I regret to tell you that 99% of the cases answer "Doctor, that is for no bad reason, I don't forget her, it is just that I walk into my office and I have so much to finish by that afternoon that I cannot distract myself". Women can be at work, do it right and pay attention to the children, the nanny, calling their mother and even plan going out with friends. Everything during the same eight hours.

This is how you can evidence that to go from one objective to another, men generally do it in a direct way, while women navigate in an endless tangle of processes. It is very common to see in therapy, with a crisis, couples that are going to get married. This happens because the bride is taking care of a thousand details, she also wants to be involved in everything, she gets tired and the bad mood and the fights start, while the groom is criticized by her because he only brings in what is asked of him and even avoids being involved in the preparation because the excess of details takes him out of focus from his other activities of his life. She takes it as "lack of interest" what is natural for him. The center of all this is that women are multi-focal – they have several targets at the same time- and they are unifocal. It is pure biology and evolution. What can be done? Understand that the best that can be done is to build a relationship based on the strengths and weaknesses of each, to make plans where she can put to use that wonderful capacity of taking care of several things at the same time and let him be the motor to provide objectivity so that things will happen in the most adequate time and method. It is a win-win agreement.

Men suffer and want to be alone; women need to suffer in company

When faced with a conflict -when they feel their worst, when they want to cry or when they experiment fear, anger or anguish- men and women react in different ways. The woman needs to be accompanied and the man needs to be alone. Because of their practical nature, centered on objectives, men need to calm down, understand what is happening to them and take action, without noise around them. Women instead, because of their nature centered on processes, they need to communicate with people who may have experienced something similar to let it out, to listen to possible options and afterwards take actions that her group supports and validates.

Both want to resolve the conflict, except that each follows a different method. If we understand this, men will know that after a fight her discomfort will go away by just listening to her, and women will understand that they need a little "time out" to cool off and solve the problem. This is not a mathematical formula. It is important to point out that I am talking about people and emotions, which means that there probably are variations in all of this, that there are also men with more feminine energy that react by calling their friends when they are heart-broken or women with great masculine energy who choose to go alone on a trip to live out their broken heart. We are subjective and that is why there are no fixed rules. I am showing you generalities.

What is right? Is it right what women or men do with their negative emotions? There is nothing correct or incorrect. There are only two different ways to face the crisis. Each one uses a different strategy. Many times, I hear couples when they tell me about their crisis and they ask me how they can end them. At the end of the story, I am aware of the fact that both are right, that there is no winner and no loser, that their brains see things in two different ways and that they don't know it. They interpret the other as indifferent or unfair and thus they cannot communicate in an assertive way.

If I have an argument with my partner and he isolates himself for a couple of hours to cool off and think, I could consider him as a coward because he is not solving the problem, or I could also consider him indifferent because he is not paying attention to my emotions, or aggressive for leaving me alone, but reality indicates that in most cases he is only isolating himself to see clearly or to forget what is happening and come back thirty minutes later as if nothing had happened. I do not expect them to give up on each other because of differences between a man and a woman, but rather I do expect them to talk about those differences and to look for a way to understand how the other one behaves in order to stop feeling that there are injustices or bad treatments.

Women are happy being needed; men are happy being heroes

Another very important difference that I have noticed in my practice and that I have also read in works of specialists on the subject is that us women are happy when we are needed, when all that mountain of things that we do help to the quality of life of the people we love. Instead, men are happy when they reach the objectives and when they know they are heroes and good providers. Why does this difference generate pain? Because women, in their effort of always being needed, she pretends to be the main and only objective in the life of her partner, and this, hardly ever happens. Once we are in a relationship with them, having achieved that objective, it is time to move to the next. This doesn't mean that once they have us, they forget us or we lose value; it only means that they lean on the tranquility of having us to keep on doing what they do best, that is, “to reach objectives”. That way, the man will be happy when he reaches his objectives and the job of the person who is by his side; to be a good partner is to support him, follow him, motivate him to move forward, make him feel like a hero, to make him feel that the changes that he is producing change her life for the better. And he must know that she will be happy when he calls her to tell her about his achievements and success and make her feel needed at that moment.

Factors that usually interfere with finding a partner

• The limiting beliefs that we bring from our childhood and adolescence concerning partners. For example, when a person believes that having a partner is something painful or that needs to be on the lookout all the time in to avoid being hurt, they will eventually enter a relationship with limitations, fears and emotions sabotaging every opportunity of having a good partner.

• A poor concept of himself / herself, that cannot be lovable or that the person is not capable of producing attraction. Within the cognitive-behavioral therapy there are two central schemes concerning beliefs that produce pain; one of them is "I am not lovable nor do I deserve love" and "I am not capable of it". Either one or the combination of the two, will convince you that relationships were not created for you to enjoy them. My recommendation is that you talk to a qualified professional and regenerate these beliefs, substituting them for others more empowering than these.

• To stay anchored in mournings of ex-partners and not closing cycles. Many people remain for years re-encountering their ex-partners both sexually or affectively and do not work the mourning correctly. The best thing you can do is to get support from people who love you and that are a retaining wall for you, activities that make you happy, besides understanding that mournings take time and space in our lives, precisely to help us heal and to be able to start again.

• Being a lonely person who doesn't like to share and meet new people. It is more and more frequent to see people who choose loneliness as the best option: "before someone hurts me, I'd better lock myself up and I don't give anybody a chance". But the true story is that in a world as dynamic as the one we live in today, where we often do not have time to interrelate with people other than family or co-workers, it is highly desirable that you open up to new activities and places, and that you make some time to meet at least one person every week. I remember there was a time when I had a patient to whom I used to say "every time you go to the dance-therapy in the park, the ideal situation is that you exchange some ideas with the person you have next to you; the task is to increase your group of friends". What for? To feel each time more comfortable in groups and to experiment what it means to leave loneliness behind.

• To have an idealized concept of your partner, that you have on your mind a set of characteristics so unreal that you cannot find anybody who has them all. This is very common and it is determined by the magic thought controlled by the media, the movies, the social networks, just to name a few. But the true story is that if you want to find someone perfect, you will never find him because perfection does not exist and if it did, it would be very boring since there wouldn't exist the possibility for growth. Put your feet upon the ground and get connected with reality; when you meet someone you feel attracted to, don't cheat yourself, look upon him as a normal person and rather pay attention to determine if he has your "non-negotiables" or not.

• To have organic sexual problems that have not been resolved and not going to the doctor to take care of them because of fear, shame or lack of knowledge, and decide to stay away from any relationship as the best possible solution. It is true that speaking about these issues with your partner in an inadequate way can hurt one's feelings, sometimes even approaching the subject very carefully can generate discomfort. However, avoiding the conversation, or even worse, not asking for help, will help destroy the relationship. Remember that sex is the basis for a good couple's relationship. This is a space that needs to be taken care of quickly and responsibly.

• To have dominant and manipulating parents who have placed us in a role of caretaker of the other. In our Latin-American culture it is very common to hear expressions like ¿ "she cannot get married because if she does, who is going to take care of me"? or, "I know that if you get married you are going to abandon me and I will have to age in a home for the elderly". In spite of scientific discoveries and the general modernization around us, we still have a large number of elderly people who will not achieve their economic and social independence expected of them, and those are the ones that become manipulative. Why? Because they did not make good decisions in their life, they did not form solid couples, nor developed skills that would make them prosper and be happy, therefore they now assume that since they did not take care of their lives, now their sons have to. My recommendation is that you work the guilt that could be caused by leaving your parents in the place that they belong, "the place of the parents", not partner, not son and much less, jailers. A healthy adult knows that a part of growing up is to deal with the not complying with other people's expectations. I am not saying that you should abandon them or hurt them, I only want you to notice when your parents are limiting you in what is normal for any adult –a life as a healthy couple, with intimacy and privacy– and take the necessary actions to be aware of their exaggerated and childish expectations thus taking care of yourself and of your lives as a couple.

To maintain ourselves in a good couple

It has nothing to do with keeping a partner next to us at whatever the cost or to count the years we have added to the anniversaries or how many children we have brought up or how many assets we have accumulated together. It is about sharing your life with that other person, generating well-being, growing and making a choice of staying together. To choose is not to bare, designate to, stand, but to choose every morning to stay with that person and do whatever is necessary so that "both" are happy through a win-win agreement.

When I share my life with another person, the first thing I must consider is when I am in a relationship that is worthed to continue and when I am only baring. This is simple; it only requires your total honesty. You must observe if 70% of your time you feel lonely, with fear, with anger, with guilt or sadness. If this is so, you definitely aren't in a healthy relationship. On the other hand, analyze if to be there you must give up your dreams and your projects, not growing and stop being yourself. And finally, the worst part, check and see if there is no trust between you two and whether one or both believe that one could intentionally hurt the other. If any one of these scenarios are the reflection of your relationship, you are in a bad and not healthy relation, which will only provide you bitterness and lower your self-esteem.

A good couple must have sex, communication and projects. In that order, because good sex opens the door to a good and fluid communication, and the good communication sets the basis to start building projects together.

Sex

When we fall in love with someone, when we start going out with someone, the first thing that attracts us is the person's looks, smells or gestures. It is very common to hear comments like "she had a beautiful smile, I loved how her hair moved, watching her walk, just hooked me up". This is what we see and joins us together, erotism, the fantasies that I construct in my mind with that person that I just saw for the first time and that I was attracted to are examples of sex making its call. But I am talking about good sex, the one that is varied, consensual, where we dare to set our fantasies free without values of judgement.

Sex is the first leg of the table that we are building and must be maintained in time through pleasure, creative erotism, intimacy and above all the real moments of love which is the post-coitus. Just as soon as pleasure and orgasm have left, it is time for both to become one and to thank each other; only then you will know if you are loving or just having sex. Those who do not try to have good sex aren't good partners, because the intimacy you can achieve in that space opens the doors to communication and the fun of the couple. Without that, boredom could appear very quickly, followed by a disconnection; at this point you will have allowed tediousness in. Inevitably, human beings need intimacy and pleasure, and if we do not find it in one place, we will look for it in another one. The bad or non-existing sex only brings unhappiness and infidelity, no doubt, one of the most serious problems faced by couples these days.

The Durex report about sexual wellness of 2012, which has studied and analyzed the habits and experiences of more than 29 thousand people in 36 countries, determined through a survey carried out by *Harris Interactive,* that even though 70% of the adults in the world consider themselves as sexually satisfied with the physical aspects of their sexual life, only 33% is "very satisfied" and 10% state that they are "totally satisfied". The most satisfied citizens of the world are in South America (72%), slightly above Europe (71%), Oceania and North America (both 68%) and Asia (67%).

Likewise, the studies on masculine and feminine infidelity have provided changing numbers throughout the years. Stephan Drigotas and William Barta indicate that in 2001- in *The Cheating Heart: Scientific Exploration of Infidelity, Current Direction in Psychological Science-* that the indicators of infidelity in individuals born between 1833 and 1942 was 37% for men and 12.4% for women, while for those born between 1953 and 1974 was 27.6% for men and 26.2% for women. The fact that both infidelity numbers are coming together for men and women has become more evident with the years and more recent studies claim that the numbers are now about even, even though the reasons for male infidelity are different from female infidelity, just as the perception that each has concerning infidelity, both in the physical setting as well as the cybersex. A more recent survey, like the one of the SexPlace franchise in Spain, claims that women are much more unfaithful than men. According to a sample of 500 persons, 52% of women claimed to have been with somebody else while being in a relationship. However, only 48% of men claim to have been unfaithful at a given point. A Spanish survey quoted by the Argentinian Psychologist Javier Martin Camacho in his book *Fidelity and infidelity in the relations of couples,* he claims to the contrary that 67% of women are unfaithful versus only 52% of men are.

Why are so many people unfaithful? What is happening? Where does this impulse to cheat and to break this agreement of exclusiveness and respect come from? I want to start by clarifying that infidelity starts by being unfaithful to oneself. If I remain in a relationship where I don't feel loved, and I justify myself with excuses, I am being immediately unfaithful with myself. And when I am doing this, my body will live it and obviously will show it because what the mind doesn't solve is suffered by the body: I will be anxious, depressed, hungry for love, my body will get sick – it is not a coincidence that we have so many women suffering of breast and uterus cancer just the same as CVA's, heart attacks in very young men - they could also go against me looking for a lover and even encouraging unconsciously that I be found out. Infidelity is a desperate scream that asks for love and attention. Why do I believe that finding a lover is to go against myself? In theory, you look for a lover because your partner doesn't love you the way you would want him to, but you will have to see this lover in hiding, half way, with guilty pleasure and that is not good for you; it may be even worse because it turns you into a worse version of yourself: a person who prefers to cheat than to resolve.

Another problem is the taboos. If you really want to maintain a good couple relationship, and if one of the two is suggesting situations with which the other does not agree, or if all contrary, no suggestions are made and boredom has gone to bed with you , then it is time to say : "we need to get the help of a sexologist or an adequate professional to improve our sexuality as a couple and to come to an agreement to introduce in our lives as much erotism and fantasies as possible".

Open yourself to the experience of looking for different things in sex.

I had a 51-year-old patient who had been in a relationship for 9 years and she was still a virgin. Yes, a virgin. Her partner was highly frustrated. She confessed that when she was thinking about oral sex, she would remember her mother who always told her that oral sex was a dirty thing, that a penetration would always cause her infections and that anal sex was only for prostitutes. She even told her that the day a man would finally take her to bed, he would leave her that same day. With those lies repeated by the mother a thousand times, this woman was incapable of letting those taboo's go and was destroying her relationship with a good man, who had also been extremely patient and caring. Her job was to revise herself as far as what is dirty, bad, inadequate and as far as considering herself valuable and worthy even enjoying good sex. If she hadn't been able to validate the rationality of her beliefs and learn over again, she would have had to let her partner go so that he could find happiness in another person. Everything is valid and acceptable, we own our own decisions, but if we want to carry on with our fears, it is not healthy to drag healthy people with us to that endless hole called infidelity.

Sex in a couple that wants to stay together must be consensual and diversified, trying a little of everything in order to decide what the couple likes from the options menu. I have seen many chaoses in couples who seemed to be well established, where the husband, laying in the same bed next to his wife, is having virtual sex with another woman through a chat. Why? What is the problem? The problem is not the other woman, nor the chat; the problem has to do with why isn't he attracted to that woman next to him? How did sex become such a routine that it seems to be more exiting to do it with another person pushing keys on a screen? or even worse, ¿why doesn't he ask his wife to experiment those things that he fantasizes with and that now he does with his "friend"?

I want to leave you here a couple of true statements that in my opinion are fundamental as far as this topic is concerned:

1. Flirting, photos, videos and sexual text messages on a chat are a form of *infidelity.*

2. Infidelity is the responsibility of both partners in a couple. It is shared. Both need to take a close look at what is causing it so that both can fix it or go their separate ways without feelings of being a victim or being victimized that would hurt their future relationships. Infidelity goes far beyond sex. If you think that infidelity only means to have sex with someone else, you are wrong. The couple' s counselor Gary Neuman reveals in his book *"The truth about cheating: why men stray and what you can do to prevent it"*, that 92% of all men confessed that they cheated

on their partners due to emotional reasons they felt disconnected or poorly appreciated by their partners. Newman's investigation indicates that an infidelity is not always related to the physical aspect; 88% of men who cheated on their wives, did it with women that they didn't consider to be more attractive than their partners.

Communication

If you are in a relationship as a couple and you do not trust your partner, if you think that she is going to hurt you, that what you tell her she is going to tell it to other people afterwards, then you are with the wrong person. Communication opens the door to many other things, but it must be transparent, without fear, without criticisms and without judgements. To be a good partner, we must understand that the other person is different, that our partner can feel, listen and give us a different opinion, and that not because of that she or he must be a bad person or not love us. An opinion is not a judgement, is not an evaluation, is not giving a grade to what someone else thinks. That is why we have to be very careful when we issue a message. We are only sharing an opinion. In any language, we must be very careful not only about what we say but also on how and when we say it. We must look for adequate moments to communicate, away from our routine and obligations. We must plan moments for communicating even though it may sound a little mechanical: it is better to do it mechanically than not do it at all. With today's fast-paced life where both partners in a couple work together both inside and outside the house, it is of vital importance to set aside a little time to nourish communication, which is the second leg of our table and without it, it is possible that everything that is on top of it would just fall to the floor.

A patient told me that he had a good communication with his partner, they told each other everything, they enjoy everything together, they laugh, they chat, but they have problems in bed and he is afraid to tell her. Communication is not only the verbal expression of emotions or to narrate actions of our day-to-day life. It is to communicate real things like honesty, intimacy, that I may not be ashamed of telling something; for example: "I am jealous of our daughter", or, "I am tired of the same position in bed". To communicate is to really say what we really want to say without minimizing our emotions.

Projects

This is the third vital piece in a real and healthy relationship. A duo that doesn't have common projects cannot be called a couple or to say the least, it cannot be called a good couple. I am not speaking of great big projects; I am talking about the next vacation, about next weekend, the next dinner together, to have a dog, anything that may be considered as a possible project by both. A project in common will keep a couple together and with energy. Many times we think it is alright that the man has his projects and the woman hers and that each one has his or her own life in the house. That is truly very healthy, but the ideal situation is that there must always be –and throughout the relationship– some project that they have in common on a day by day basis. That will keep them connected and following up on each other to reach an objective and at the end they will have a success in common to celebrate.

A study carried out by the *National Opinion Research Center* in 2010, showed that women are 40% more prone to cheat on their partners, when compared with the data from past decades. Some investigators relate this increase to the recent independence of women and their trips with friends and without their partners. That is, projects and finances go separate ways in the couple.

There are people who claim not to have projects in common and they do not appreciate that a simple bar-b-que can be a project for which they have to plan, or what they would do for Mother's Day, or how they would paint the house. The project doesn't mean great things. Pick something that you can plan together every week; this will allow the couple to work on something in the present looking at the future. The love in a couple brings them closer and not having common projects produces resentment.

Those destructive "should"

When it isn't consensual, the words "you should" become aggressive. Every time I start or end a conversation with those words, it means that there was no conversation but an aggression. The expression "you should" is like a nose. We all have one but they are all different, because they come from my growing up, my life, my history. Among the most important reasons for which couples split up is because they do not generate enough "shoulds" together. One "should" as a result of an agreement between the two partners in a couple, can be very positive, especially when they decide to do something without any major arguments. For example, if we are talking about moving and it is good for everybody, or changing schools or eating healthier.

The "shoulds" are beliefs and orders that we bring from home and that we want to impose to the person we are going to be with. These "shoulds" must be talked over calmly but the people who have bad couple relationships only talk about this when they are arguing and that is why they cannot come to any agreements.

When two persons decide to live together, the first thing they must care for is mutual respect, accepting the new habits and the flexibility to create new routines that prove to be beneficial for both and without all those bothersome and unexplainable "shoulds".

There are many situations in which the "shoulds" can destroy a couple's relationship. I will tell you here about the ones that most frequently occur:

Managing of money

If I used the "shoulds" of my own house, the ones from the Carrillo Monagas family, ¿who would be willing to marry me if I said that the man of the house "should" pay for everything, absolutely everything? I am sure that nobody would, because my "should" resembles more an attack than anything else. If it were the other way around, if somebody wanted to marry me and said that we "should" both pay for everything, I would consider it as something offensive and would look upon that man as someone stingy and cheap. In time and with the blows I have endured in my life and finally with my divorce, I have learned that the best way to manage the household expenses -because money is a very strong energy in a relationship -is to create some kind of account where each partner can contribute with his/her income and where a certain percentage is left for each partner to be spent at will. This is not the only way to do it, there are many more. What is important is that whichever is chosen must be the result of an agreement.

Even though it is true that money is a necessary element and that without it is almost imposible to live, it is also true that if we learn certain managing rules, we can turn it into an allied to help us with the well-being of our relations. Maybe at the beginning of a romance this is a taboo subject and it would seem something you just don't talk about, but if we are thinking of a medium to long-term relationship, this topic should be taken into account as soon as possible.

It has become more and more frequent to hear phrases in my practice like "my wife spends too much, she is not conscious of our budget", or, "he is very stingy but he always buys electronic toys and a new car every year", "if there isn't enough money for our home, there won't be money for her mother either", or, "we will end up on the street if he/she keeps on spending our savings".

First of all, I would recommend a quiet conversation where each would express his/her point of view as to how to manage the couple's finances. This will allow them to know about the beliefs that the other partner has on this subject based on his/her education and previous experiences. In second place, it would be ideal to create a list of all fixed expenses involved in living together: rent, utilities, going out, food, insurance, etcetera. With this information they would have a very good idea of the means necessary in order for each to have what is needed as well as well-being. In third place, it must be decided how these expenses will be paid. Whether all the money goes into an individual account and payments are made from there or if it will be divided in percentages, for example, 50% each, because it is probable that one makes more money than the other, or if everything will be paid by the partner with the higher income.

Once these three points are clear, they would be ready to go deeper in the relationship if they are interested in a committed, stable and with long-term expenses such as mortgages and children. These are topics that should be very well agreed upon, because these commitments should contemplate the possibility that one of the two is left without a job or even the possibility that they get divorced. If it is possible, they must also decide at that moment if they both want to sign a pre-nuptial agreement, taking into account that this doesn't mean that they love each other any less. The idea is that money should make their lives and their life as a couple a better place to be in and not a space for fights and disputes.

Money is an uncomfortable subject but it is something that has to be talked about so that nothing is assumed without an agreement and that we do not generate too many "shoulds".

Friends. ¿Are they untouchable?

Friends have a place in the history of our life. If someone offends them, we are offended too. If someone wants to eliminate them, they do it unto us as well. Friends are a part of the non-negotiable "shoulds". A woman that makes her husband stay away from his friends is disrespecting that man and also abusing him. And how does a man defend himself from such abuse? Abusing and mistreating her, maybe ignoring her or getting a more fun and less critical lover for himself.

Many couples have problems because a barbecue with his friends or a simple going out with her friends make the other feel left alone. The private life of each person belongs to each person; what is important is that when we get together with someone as a couple, we must know how to set a separate space for friends and another for the family. There must be at least one weekend for friends, to share time with them who are happy people who do us good. Another weekend must be for the family, because without a family – when you have one – there is no partner and without a partner there is no family. There is space for everyone in our lives, and if there isn't it must be found.

Technology. Does it have a limit?

It is very difficult nowadays not to use the social networks and technological devices, but are we aware of their danger as far as making us work more, and above all, how alone we leave our partner. Many get home and are connected until midnight, we empower the social networks when we pay too much attention to what other people say, to the virtual life of our ex-partners, to all those chats where we get emotionally connected with people who are not our partners, which in turn becomes one of the forms of infidelity.

The use of social media must be discussed and established in the couple, otherwise we will see vengeance make her appearance. And the rules for this cannot come in the form of a "should" but rather in the form of a mutual understanding.

Work

When the job of one of the partners implies taking work to be done at home or when a person who works from home must keep on doing it in non-conventional schedules, some problems arise that affect relationships very much. It is important to ask yourself at what time does the working schedule end and define, according to the needs, the limits to leave work out of the family and partner space.

Those who are going to live together, must previously establish how many emergencies they are willing to tolerate, or how late they are going to work or take care of third parties.

I met a couple where the man arrived at home from work at 5 pm, but he would get connected at 9 pm; by then, the kids were already sleeping and his wife was tired. It is fundamental to remember our partner must be looked upon like a team in order to be like a healthy family and at the same time pay all the bills, and that there is no competition to see who works more or who makes more money.

House chores

The house chores issue is one of the most frequent reasons for disputes and separations. A way to minimize conflicts is to prepare a list of all the things that need to be done in the household and another list with the likes and capabilities of each one to see how the chores will be allocated. When there are chores that we don't like to do, we can share the chores in days. Many times, it is felt that the partner who takes care of the housework doesn't get the deserved recognition –"nobody noticed all I did today"– while the work done in the street always has a higher significance. Even when a person works outside all day, this partner must share some of the house chores.

Your family and my family

This is a very sore and algid issue. In general, when we get married, we are leaving our original families to which we have been tied up emotionally. This causes that at the beginning of leaving as a couple there is a lot of interaction with the parents in law, brothers, our respective families: this isn't always natural and comfortable. My maternal grandparents, for example, always had keys to my house and my father accepted it well, but I have noticed that this doesn't always work well. It is important from the beginning to establish the time and space parameters for our new family. The limit is the one each partner imposes. We must ask ourselves how much time should we share with the families of both partners, since in general, when one or both families are much too involved with the couple and their new family, it is because the subject wasn't previously discussed enough. When we create the "should", it is better to establish the rules: indicate the times of arrival, weekend restrictions, among other things.

I had a patient whose mother in law had the keys to their house, she would come in without calling first and would do all the laundry. In her mind it was something well done and help, but the daughter in law did not understand it that way; she did not like the way their clothes were done and she took that action as a continuous intromission. There never was a conversation to specify the limits the couple would establish upon third parties regarding the coexistence space of the couple.

Raising of the children and discipline

This is another cause for divorce. It is about revising the things that will be allowed at home and the limits and rules of co-existence. I remember a couple that used to tell me that every time the son wanted something, since the grandmother had more authority than the father, they always wound up doing what the son wanted. It is the children who have no rules or good manners who become tyrants. And all of that was caused because the parents never sat down to talk about what is best for the children at each age. It is not the same a "should" for a three-year-old child than for an adolescent. When a member of the couple is frequently in favor of the son, but the other is not, serious problems appear which lead directly to a divorce.

Appendix 3

Make a list of the "shoulds" that you constantly impose upon others ______________________________

____

____

Make a list of the "shoulds" that you let other people impose on you ______________________________

____

____

Which "shoulds" do you consider that you need to keep in your life? Why and what for? __________

____

____

Which "shoulds" do you need to get rid of starting today? Why and what for? ______________

____

____

What have you noticed writing down the above information? ______________________________

____

____

Alerts criteria to maintain the couple

If I don't stop at the red traffic lights when I drive my car, and I run three red lights and nothing happens, it is very likely that when I run the fourth red light, I will suffer a crash. The traffic lights function as an alert sign, just like the criteria and some "shoulds" that we use with our partner. Those criteria must be displayed in visible places: the refrigerator, the bathroom door or the closet. That way, just like we frequently check our car, we must check those criteria to give maintenance to our relationship as a couple. Everyone writes on a list what is indispensable in order for the couple to keep functioning.

The alert criteria have to do with the permanent revisions that I do about my life and they are not a task that is done one day only; we need to pay attention to these points up to the last minute of our lives I we want to be everyday a better version of ourselves. It has to do with being alert when certain messages appear because they say a lot about us:

• You guide and evaluate your relationship based on your parents' experience:

Those things that you bring from home and that you haven't modified, those that make you point at the person who thinks, feels or acts different from you. To be with another person is a decision and if that person does not function for us or doesn't turn out to be a good combination with us, we have the option of leaving even though we love that person. What is not right is to accuse her and judge her because she doesn't do things the way your parents did in their home.

• You do not observe yourself and you look for responsibilities outside of yourself:

A healthy couple sits down to speak and recognizes everyone's responsibilities. When a person doesn't observe him/herself, it becomes very difficult to know his/her positive and negative points, and when this happens it is also difficult to connect with a partner and there is no empathy. Without empathy and a connection, we cannot be genuine persons and thus we will not be able to get involved and really love others. We need to lose fear and recognize our errors and admit them. We are not perfect; we are in permanent construction. Until we are ready to admit this, we will not feel worthy of showing our virtues and share them with others.

• **You have an ideal partner model, not anchored on reality; stop looking for perfection.**

Human beings are imperfect, we have no warranties or labels indicating expiration dates. If you want a relationship as a couple to last twenty years, stop thinking how long it is going to last. The fact that nobody knows whether we are going to be alive tomorrow morning makes it that we cannot find warranties or certainties in our relations as a couple. Humanize those who surround you. Set priorities: we cannot have it all. Enjoy what you have. Many people get lost in the present because they are constantly analyzing what could happen and they become history. Obviously, planning for the future is important but don't base your life on that, and even less your life as a couple, because all spontaneity is lost too, attached to a result produces anxiety. Live "as if" in your story you were the person that always comes out ahead and finds a way to solve whatever turns up. Who would you be if you stopped putting together terror movies in your mind? Surely a happy person: get used to that.

• You apply the use of control and surveillance over your partner.

If you find yourself checking, controlling, interrogating, is because you don't feel well loved. The problem is not the other person, but a wrong type of communication. Whoever is too well informed about her partner, because she follows him and checks him, only has a false sensation of control. It is a simple form of distraction. Besides, he/she plays to be the mother or father which "kills" erotism because healthy people do not have sex with their mother or father.

• You do not observe or reinforce what your partner does well.

Good partners are present and attentive at the right moment to reinforce what their partners do well. We know that we simply tend to ignore every wrong conduct that wants to be eliminated; in the context of couples, to ignore what hurts us does not solve conflicts. Somebody used to tell me "It is her turn to cook on Wednesdays; I got up early and cleaned so that she would happily cook, but after half an hour she calls me to tell me that I left my towel in the bathroom". This person did not reinforce the positive action but rather concentrated her attention on a small negative event. The complaint "you never do anything right" darkens all other actions that were done adequately and with a good intention.

- **You victimize yourself.**

Many times, we want the other person to change his/her way of living and thinking so that they can be with us, and it just so happens that the person already changed and doesn't want to be in a couple relationship with us or doesn't have the time or space to be in a relationship as a couple. It is important to know if there is time and space in your life for someone else, because if you do not take care of that person you already know what is going to happen. When you find yourself frequently criticizing your partner, check and see if it is really that person who is no good and think what you are going to do about that with what you have learned, or come to the conclusion that you are the one who is not ready for a couple relationship.

Some people become addicts to the insane sensation of anger, mistrust and rematch, when finally, one day they take charge and go to a good therapist and have the life they always dreamed of, they begin to feel the need of the drug of conflict. They need their doses of unhappiness and start with a new imaginary problem. They ask themselves: "and if that happiness is a lie? or, ¿ "and if he is only faking a change?", or, "what if he is planning to leave me?"

¿Can your partner leave you? Yes, there is always a possibility, every day. Worry about that but whenever if happens, do not anticipate it, don't waste what you have achieved after so much suffering. Don't waste the good present you have today with your partner. Live!

- **Repeating routines that wear off the relationship.**

You must be attentive and consciously reduce those routines that we know destroy the relationship. In one occasion, I heard the sons of a couple talking about how terrible it was to celebrate mother's day with their parents: every year they would get up, it took them forever to get ready, they left very hungry a couple of hours later, they drove around in their car looking for a restaurant to "celebrate", but since that day all restaurants are very busy and they had not booked a reservation -they never did- then it would take them another couple of hours to be able to sit in a good place to eat, and by then we were all very tired, in a bad mood and hungry due to the long wait, and thus, the supposed to be celebration ended up being a nightmare. If that couple wanted to keep their relationship healthy, they would change that routine. The following year, as they got up, they would have breakfast to get ready without rush and went out to a place for which they had booked a reservation. That way, both the ride as well as the celebration itself would have been a good excuse to celebrate as a family and not a torture from which we all would like to run away from. Many times, small changes are necessary; you just need to dedicate the right attention.

To take notes

How do I know when I am in a good couple relationship? When I pay attention to those alarm criteria and I can say that I am another person's friend and I want everything to go well for that person, when I wish happiness to that person and that all objectives come true, to please that person in bed, to have common projects, that I want to do everything within my reach to make that person's day always better every day I wake up in the morning.

Healthy love

John Gottman and Nan Silver carried out an investigation at Washington University that after sixteen years and the participation of thousands of couples, generated one of the most beautiful concepts of love I have ever seen. Investigators point out that healthy love is experimented by couples who share a deep friendship who intimately know each other, who know their tastes, personalities, hopes and dreams, who show consideration for each other and express their love with daily small details.

Close your eyes and check how do you connect with healthy love. Ask yourself if the person who is your couple:

- Is there with you in good times and bad times?
- Is always willing to negotiate differences?
- Does that person accept you the way you are?
- Doesn't need you, but even then, stays beside you?
- Feels happy with him/herself and with you?

- Does he/she give to you and enjoys it?
- Does he/she pamper you, takes care of you and gives you pleasure in bed?
- Does he/she enjoy the same things you do?
- Does he/she point out your mistakes in a lovely and dedicated way?

If you have a partner and you see yourself reflected with positive answers in all of the above-mentioned questions, thank yourself, thank your partner and enjoy life. If you don't find positive answers to those questions, check yourself in order to change the situation. Stop accumulating doubts, you should accumulate moments. Look for a partner your size.

Am I a good partner?

We attract what we are, what we receive is a function of what we honestly give. I want to put special emphasis on the word "honestly", because it isn't only about what I give but about what I honestly give.

We possess in terms of what we believe we deserve. Then, ¿what am I looking for now? ¿Am I looking for someone who will make me happy or someone to make happy? ¿Someone who will give me love or someone in whom deposit my love? To be a good partner can be summarized in just one phrase: I am a good partner when I am looking for someone to give him/her my happiness and share my growth with him/her.

When you leave this world, that person who was your partner is not going to remember what you bought together nor how much time you gave her; she is going to remember how you made her feel during your relationship as a couple.

Life is made for us to be happy most of the time, laugh, enjoy, dance, make love and be successful. However, everything has a price; you must be willing to pay the price of knowing you, loving you, to have a clear list of what for you is not negotiable and to maintain a firm position on that and not giving in under any circumstances; the price of being capable of spending some time in loneliness while you change your irrational ways of living and if someone does turn up that really wants to be with you and wants to complement your life.

Happiness will remain longer with you when you are able to say with all sureness and conviction "I love you but I don't need you", when you stop having relationships where the control, manipulation and fear are the main actors. Happiness will remain by your side when you internalize that "loving" is wonderful while "having to love" is terrible.

Let's get our present back, let's stop thinking about the future, that the couple relationship has to last and that it has to be good. Let's stop thinking about the past and of the times that the couples you had hurt you. Let's concentrate on this moment that is the only thing we have. Our productive and enjoyable life is short: we don't live beyond eighty or ninety. ¿And when is it that we begin to enjoy life?

When is it that we start learning? ¿and when is it that we begin to love? It can be any day; the difference lies in realizing that this is for a limited time. Our only resource –and it isn't renewable– is time: therefore, go out and find a person like you in the essential points, who shares your beliefs, who has fun in the things you like, who loves your jokes and who is willing to be with you in your moments of sadness. As of today, as soon as you drop this book, you will have within you the tools to be in a constant revision and to be a good partner.

Happiness does not lie in achieving the ideal "me" but in the process of travelling towards it without despising yourself and without anxiety.

Walter Riso

Belkis Carrillo

Psychologist graduated from The Metropolitan University in Caracas Venezuela. Belkis Carrillo has a diploma in Cognitive-Conductual Therapy with special studies in Emotional Rational Therapy in the Flores University in Argentina. She is an announcer and collaborator of several magazines as well as radio and television shows. She had an outstanding performance in her Master's Degree in Hypnotherapy (Flicah School – Miami, Florida) and her Master's Degree in Sexology, Education and Sexual Consulting (Alcala University in Madrid, Spain). She has achieved extensive work and experience in all of these areas.

ONLINE PSICOTHERAPY

New technologies have changed the way we interact, communicate and exchange information with other people. It is now possible to carry out a quality psychological therapy from your house or office through internet, or if you prefer it, through the phone.

IN PERSON COACHING OR ONLINE

Through coaching, the coach instructs persons so that by using their own abilities they can reach their objectives in an efficient way. In the process specific objectives are established and an action plan is designed in order to achieve those objectives in the specified time.

CONFERENCES, CONVERSATIONALS AND TALKS

An encounter designed for those who feel the need to learn about love, in order to have them become conscious of their strengths and weaknesses, so that they could find and maintain healthy relations that will provide them well-being.

PRIVATE MEETINGS

This is a type of encounter designed for a maximum of 10 participants, who in a close and intimate environment, choose a subject of interest to be developed using the doubts and questions that each person may have.

Index

This edition of
*How Can I be a
good partner?* by
Belkis Carrillo,
was done by
Plan B editorial©
In Caracas,
Venezuela, in April
2017.

Made in United States
Orlando, FL
28 May 2022

18257127R00109